The Wealth Delusion

How Money and Power Distort the Mind

Paul Green, M.Ed.

The information in this book is intended for educational and informational purposes only. It is not intended to constitute medical, psychological, legal, or financial advice. Readers should consult qualified professionals before acting on any information contained herein.

The research and case studies discussed in this book are drawn from publicly available peer-reviewed sources, news reporting, and published accounts. All citations are provided in the Notes section. The author has made every effort to ensure accuracy; any errors are unintentional.

References to real companies and public figures are made for illustrative and educational purposes only.

First Edition

ISBN: [Paperback] 978-1-966703-28-0

Abstract

THE WEALTH DELUSION

How Money and Power Distort the Mind

Paul Green, M.Ed.

This book examines the documented psychological and neurological effects of extreme wealth accumulation and concentrated institutional power on the human beings who experience them. Drawing on peer-reviewed research in neuroscience, social psychology, organizational behavior, developmental psychology, and behavioral economics, it proposes a six-stage synthesis (the Wealth Insanity Cycle) that connects distinct bodies of research into a coherent account of how

and why extreme wealth and power reliably produce specific cognitive, behavioral, and moral outcomes.

Topics addressed include: dopamine dysregulation and wealth-seeking behavior; the neurological effects of sustained power on perspective-taking and empathy; the organizational dynamics that select for psychopathic trait profiles; historical patterns of elite behavioral distortion; the mechanisms of moral disengagement; the psychology of entitlement; the intersection of power and sexual behavior; the architecture of philanthropic reputation management; intergenerational transmission of psychological dysfunction in dynastic wealth; practical strategies for individuals in proximity to these dynamics; and the structural policy interventions supported by the evidence base.

The book is intended for general adult readers and draws on more than sixty peer-reviewed citations. It is not a work of political advocacy but of evidence synthesis, and its analysis applies regardless of the political affiliation of the powerful individuals and institutions it examines.

Keywords: wealth psychology | power and cognition | corporate psychopathy | hubris syndrome | moral disengagement | empathy erosion | DARVO | inequality | systemic reform | behavioral economics

Table of Contents

Introduction

The Most Polite Way to Say What Everyone Is Already Thinking

"The first time someone calls you a horse, punch them in the nose. The second time, think about it. The third time, buy a saddle."

Let's start with what this book is not: It is not a screed. It is not class warfare dressed up in footnotes. It is not the work of someone who is angry about being poor, because the author is not poor. It is not the kind of book that uses the word 'oligarchy' fourteen times per chapter while offering no mechanism for how or why the patterns it describes actually work. It is not asking you to be outraged. It is asking you to pay attention to what the research says, because the research is considerably more interesting, and considerably more damning, than the outrage alone.

Here is what this book actually is: it is the peer-reviewed case for something millions of people have noticed, experienced firsthand, and then been told was either their imagination or their politics. The case that concentrated wealth and institutional power do something specific, documentable, and largely predictable to the human beings who accumulate them. That the behavioral patterns most of us have observed in wealthy and powerful people are not random. They are not coincidence. They have mechanisms, those mechanisms have names, and the names are in the scientific literature where they have been sitting, largely unread by general audiences, for decades.

The title of this book is deliberately chosen. 'Delusion' is not a casual insult; it is a clinical term for a fixed belief maintained despite contradictory evidence, and it describes with uncomfortable precision what the research documents: a pattern of distorted thinking, broken feedback loops, and systematically incorrect self-assessment that concentrated wealth and power reliably produce. The word surfaces when you watch a person with more resources than they could spend in a hundred lifetimes explain, with apparent sincerity, that they simply cannot afford to pay their employees a living wage. It fits when you observe someone donate a hospital wing with their name on it and simultaneously lobby against the healthcare policies that would make hospitals less necessary. It captures something real about the cognitive dissonance, the spectacular empathy failures, and the moral accounting tricks that the research documents in detail.

If the framing still bothers you, substitute 'demonstrably impaired in specific and predictable ways.' The science is the same. The title just fits better on a cover.

Why This Book, Why Now

The wealth gap between the very rich and everyone else has been documented with increasing precision over the past two decades. Thomas Piketty's Capital in the Twenty-First Century (2014) gave the general public a 700-page empirical history of wealth concentration and where it tends to lead when left unaddressed. Emmanuel Saez and Gabriel Zucman's ongoing research program has produced an increasingly granular map of who owns what, how that's changed, and what policy instruments have historically moved the distribution. The economic case for concern about extreme wealth concentration is well-established and growing.

What has been less synthesized for a general audience is the psychological and neuroscientific parallel track: what happens inside the human beings at the top of those concentration curves. This is the gap this book is trying to fill. Not 'here is why inequality is bad for society': that case has been made, repeatedly, by people far more qualified in macroeconomics than I am. **But rather:** here is what the research shows happens to the specific humans involved in generating and perpetuating that inequality, why those outcomes are predictable rather than coincidental, and what it means for the rest of us that the people making decisions with the most consequences for everyone are also the people most reliably affected by the patterns described here.

The research is not new. The dopamine dysregulation work has been building since the 1990s. Lord David Owen published on hubris syndrome in 2007. The corporate psychopathy literature has been accumulating for two decades. Jennifer Freyd coined DARVO in 1997. Suniya Luthar's research on affluent youth began in the late 1990s. Thomas Gilovich's work on entitlement, Dacher Keltner's on power and the reduction of prosocial behavior, Paul Piff's on social class and ethical behavior; this is an established body of work, published in peer-reviewed journals, replicated across populations and contexts, and largely inaccessible to anyone who doesn't have a university library login and a tolerance for academic prose.

The synthesis is what's new. The argument that these bodies of research are describing the same phenomenon from different angles: that the neuroscience, the social psychology, the organizational behavior research, the developmental psychology, and the policy research all converge on a coherent picture of what concentrated wealth and power reliably do to human beings. That synthesis is what this book is attempting.

This book is not asking you to be outraged. The outrage will take care of itself. It is asking you to understand the mechanism, because you cannot fix what you cannot name.

The Framework: The Wealth Insanity Cycle

Before we begin the chapters, it's worth naming the shape of what we're looking at.

The research in this book is not eleven separate studies about eleven separate problems. It is one phenomenon, documented from eleven different angles by researchers who often don't cite each other because they work in different disciplines. Neuroscientists study dopamine. Social psychologists study power. Organizational behaviorists study corporate culture. Developmental psychologists study affluent youth.

They are all, it turns out, describing the same machine.

Call it the Wealth Insanity Cycle. It has six stages. They don't always appear in the same order, and a person can enter the cycle at any stage, but they tend to reinforce each other in a sequence that is now well-documented in the literature.

Here is how it works:

STAGE 1: DOPAMINE CAPTURE. Wealth accumulation activates the brain's reward circuitry in ways that are functionally similar to addiction. The more money arrives, the more the system recalibrates its baseline, requiring ever-larger rewards to produce the same satisfaction. The pursuit becomes compulsive not because of greed in the moralistic sense, but because the neural architecture has been restructured.

STAGE 2: POWER POISONING. As wealth produces institutional power, a second neurological process begins. Power suppresses the mirror neuron systems responsible for reading other people's emotional states. The powerful person literally becomes less able to perceive, and therefore less likely to respond to, the inner lives of others. This is not metaphorical. It is measurable in brain imaging studies.

STAGE 3: PSYCHOPATHIC SELECTION. The behavioral profile produced by Stages 1 and 2 (charm, risk tolerance, reduced empathy, compulsive pursuit) : it is precisely the profile

that institutional hierarchies select for and reward. The corporate ladder does not produce psychopathic traits. It identifies people who already have them and promotes them preferentially. The result is a concentration of these traits at the top of most major institutions.

STAGE 4: EMPATHY EROSION. Extended exposure to power, combined with the social insulation that wealth provides, accelerates the degradation of empathic attunement. Wealthy people increasingly inhabit environments in which everyone around them is financially incentivized to agree, accommodate, and protect rather than challenge, correct, or inform. The feedback loops that maintain normal social cognition in the rest of us have been systematically removed.

STAGE 5: MORAL DISENGAGEMENT. As empathy erodes, the psychological mechanisms that make ethical behavior feel necessary also weaken. Bandura's moral disengagement framework documents the specific cognitive moves: moral justification, diffusion of responsibility, dehumanization of victims, and displacement of blame, that allow people to commit or enable harm while maintaining a self-concept of basic decency. These mechanisms are not unique to wealthy people, but they are activated more frequently and more successfully when power insulates a person from the consequences of using them.

STAGE 6: SYSTEM CAPTURE. The endpoint of the cycle is institutional. Individuals who have

moved through the preceding five stages do not simply accumulate personal dysfunction. They reshape the organizations, regulatory systems, and cultural narratives around them to protect and perpetuate the conditions that produced them. Philanthropy becomes reputation management. Political donations become regulatory capture. Cultural influence becomes the manufacturing of consent for arrangements that benefit a small number of people at significant cost to everyone else. The cycle doesn't just damage individuals. It reproduces itself.

The Wealth Insanity Cycle is not speculative. It is a synthesis of six documented research programs, viewed together. Each chapter of this book examines one stage of the cycle in depth. By the end, you will be able to see the whole machine.

A few important caveats before we proceed. The cycle describes a pattern and a direction, not a deterministic sentence. Not everyone who accumulates wealth moves through all six stages. Not everyone who reaches Stage 3 reaches Stage 6. Protective factors exist: maintained social connections outside wealthy circles, deliberate accountability structures, genuine rather than performative exposure to the consequences of one's decisions, and the research identifies them. The cycle is what happens when those protective factors are absent. In environments of extreme wealth concentration, they tend to be.

The cycle is also not a closed loop from which there is no exit. Chapter Ten is about how individuals can interrupt it at the interpersonal level. Chapter

Eleven is about how policy can interrupt it at the structural level. The fact that the cycle is documented does not mean it is inevitable. It means it is a known system, operating by known mechanisms, which can therefore (unlike ignorance, unlike coincidence) actually be addressed.

Now let's look at each stage.

A Note on Scope and Fairness

The research in this book describes tendencies, probabilities, and structural pressures, not universal laws that apply to every wealthy person without exception. The literature on power and empathy documents that power tends to reduce prosocial behavior and empathy on average. It does not document that every powerful person becomes less empathetic. The literature on entitlement and moral disengagement documents a reliable association between high socioeconomic status and elevated ethical infractions in experimental settings. It does not document that every wealthy person cheats, rationalizes harm, or treats rules as decorative.

There are wealthy people who do not exhibit the patterns this book describes. Some of them work deliberately against the structural conditions that produce those patterns. They are not the modal case in the research literature, but they are real, and acknowledging their existence is not courtesy; it is analytical accuracy. The goal of this book is not to establish that all wealthy people are irredeemably damaged. The goal is to establish that the systems producing and maintaining extreme wealth concentration reliably produce specific psychological outcomes, that those outcomes are well-documented, and that a society interested in its own functioning has both the evidence and the mechanism to address the conditions generating them.

The book is also not a political document in the partisan sense. The research on power disinhibition applies equally to liberal and conservative billionaires, Democratic megadonors and Republican ones, tech founders whose politics lean left and oil executives whose politics lean right. Hubris syndrome does not check voter registration. Neither does the dopamine dysregulation associated with extreme wealth accumulation. The structural critique in the final chapter argues for policy changes that have historically been associated with center-left politics, but the empirical case for those changes is grounded in evidence rather than ideology, and the research it draws on is published in peer-reviewed journals without partisan affiliation.

How to Use This Book

The chapters are designed to build on each other but can also be read independently if you're the kind of person who reads the chapter about power and sex first. No judgment. That's Chapter Seven.

Chapters One through Four establish the foundations: the neuroscience of money and dopamine, the psychology of power and its effects on cognition, the organizational dynamics that select for specific personality profiles, and the historical pattern showing these dynamics are not modern inventions. Chapters Five through Nine go deeper on specific mechanisms: empathy erosion, entitlement and moral disengagement, the intersection of power and sexual behavior, the philanthropy architecture, and the intergenerational transmission of psychological dysfunction along with dynastic wealth.

Chapter Ten is the field guide: the practical toolkit for people who are currently in professional or personal proximity to the dynamics this book describes and need something more immediately useful than institutional critique. DARVO recognition. The gray rock method. Documentation strategy. Exit planning. That chapter can be read first if your situation is urgent.

Chapter Eleven is the systemic chapter: what structural change looks like, what the historical and international precedents show, and what the graded action list looks like from individual consumer choices to organized political participation. It is the chapter that answers the question every well-researched problem book has an obligation to answer: okay, so what do we actually do?

The research notes at the end of each chapter are for readers who want to go to the primary sources. The argument of this book is that you should. The peer-reviewed literature on these topics is richer, stranger, and more disturbing than any summary can fully convey. The citations are not decoration. They are an invitation.

One last thing before we start.

If you have picked up this book because someone in your life (a boss, a parent, a spouse, a founder, a colleague, a politician) has been doing things that made no sense to you, things that seemed inexplicable given their resources and their stated values and their apparent intelligence, things that you were told were your problem to manage rather than their problem to address: you were not imagining it. The patterns are real. The mechanisms are documented. You were not confused because you were wrong. You were confused because no one had handed you the framework yet.

Here it is. ☺

Chapter 1

Your Brain on Money

Brad used to be normal.

He coached Little League on Saturday mornings and complained about the umpires in exactly the way Little League dads do: loudly, briefly, then forgotten by the parking lot. He brought his trash cans in on the right day. When the family next door had a water pipe burst in February, Brad was the one who showed up at 11 PM with a shop vac and didn't ask for anything in return. If you had to describe Brad in a single word, the word would be fine. Not extraordinary. Not terrible. Solid human being.

Then Brad won the lottery.

Not the nice kind where you replace the refrigerator and take the family to Disney. Brad won $400 million. The kind of number where the math stops working for normal people, where you can no longer trace a line from the amount to any recognizable human need it might satisfy. Four hundred million dollars. You could fund a small country's education budget. You could buy an island. You could, as Brad eventually did, buy several things we're legally unable to describe in full without triggering a nondisclosure agreement.

Within eighteen months, Brad had a staff. Within three years, he had a jet. Within five years, the third home in Europe he referenced constantly and unnecessarily. Within seven years, Brad had stopped returning calls from people he had known his entire life. He no longer remembered why he'd found the Little League umpires funny. He found, increasingly, that other people's problems registered as noise rather than signal.

Within ten years, Brad was on the news for reasons involving a yacht, a different nondisclosure agreement, and the phrase 'mutual departure from an untenable situation.'

People who had known Brad for decades shook their heads and said the same thing: money revealed who he really was. A bad person hiding in a good person's clothes.

The neuroscience says something considerably stranger.

Money didn't reveal Brad. Money changed Brad's brain. Not metaphorically. Not as shorthand for 'corrupted his values.' The money, the power, and the status that followed it rewired his neural circuitry at a biological level, shifting how he processes reward, how he reads other people's emotions, how much he cares about consequences, and, eventually, how much he is neurologically capable of caring about you at all.

And Brad is not unusual. Brad is the documented case. Brad has been replicated in labs, measured in brain scanners, and observed in field studies at intersections in the San Francisco Bay Area. Brad is not a warning. Brad is a finding.

Here is what the research says happened to him.

What happened to Brad?

Brad didn't change his values, exactly. Brad didn't suddenly decide to become a different person. What happened to Brad is something far more interesting, far more disturbing, and far more documented by neuroscientists than you might expect: Brad's brain changed. The money, the power, the status: they didn't just change Brad's circumstances. They rewired Brad's neural circuitry at a biological level, shifting how he processes other people, how he responds to reward, how much he cares about consequences, and frankly, how much he cares about you.

This chapter is about that process. It's about what actually happens inside the brain when wealth and power accumulate: what it does to the dopamine system, what it does to empathy, and why the richest man in the room isn't the happiest, or the wisest, or the most ethical. He's just the most thoroughly medicated by his own neurochemistry.

And the science, it turns out, is damning.

The Dopamine Trap: Why They Can Never Have Enough

Before we talk about rich people specifically, we need to talk about dopamine, because understanding dopamine is the key to understanding why extreme wealth behaves more like a chronic disease than a lifestyle upgrade.

Dopamine is the brain's primary motivation molecule. Not pleasure exactly; that's a common misconception. Dopamine is more accurately described as the brain's "wanting" chemical, the neurological signal that says “go get that thing, it’s important.” It’s what makes you reach for your phone, pursue a promotion, crave sugar at 11pm, and compulsively refresh your email even though nothing good has ever arrived at 11pm.

Here’s the part that matters: dopamine is driven more by the anticipation of reward than by the reward itself. The seeking is the high. The getting is almost beside the point.

Researcher Kent Berridge at the University of Michigan spent years studying this distinction, separating what he called the brain’s “wanting” system (driven by dopamine, which creates craving and pursuit) from the “liking” system (driven by opioid circuits, which produces actual satisfaction). His findings revealed something crucial: the wanting system is significantly more powerful than the liking system. You can want something desperately that you won’t actually enjoy very much when you get it. And here’s the kicker: you tend to seek more than you are ever satisfied.

Now apply that to wealth accumulation.

Every business deal closed, every stock gain, every zero added to a net worth: these trigger dopamine release in the brain’s reward circuits, particularly in the nucleus accumbens and the ventral tegmental area. The brain marks these events as important, rewarding, worth repeating. The pursuit becomes a neurological imperative. And like any dopamine-driven behavior, tolerance builds. What used to produce a significant dopamine response starts requiring more input to generate the same effect. The first million is thrilling. The tenth is just Tuesday. The hundredth requires a rocket ship, apparently.

Sam Bankman-Fried (known universally as SBF) built FTX into one of the world's largest cryptocurrency exchanges in approximately three years. By 2022, he was worth an estimated $26 billion. He appeared on the covers of financial magazines. He was photographed with former presidents and current senators. He testified before Congress. He ran an effective altruism operation that pledged to give most of his fortune away. He was, by the account of essentially everyone who covered him, one of the most brilliant allocators of risk in the history of financial markets.

He was also, it turned out, running one of the largest financial frauds in American history.

When FTX collapsed in November 2022, approximately $8 billion in customer funds were missing. The money had been used, through Bankman-Fried's affiliated trading firm, Alameda Research, to fund speculative trades, political donations, luxury real estate in the Bahamas, and various other expenditures that had nothing to do with the customers who had deposited it. Bankman-Fried was arrested in December 2022 and convicted of fraud and conspiracy charges in October 2023. He was sentenced to 25 years in federal prison.

The FTX case is important for this chapter not primarily because of the fraud (fraud has many motivations and mechanisms. It's important because of what Bankman-Fried's own accounts reveal about the psychology of someone operating inside Stage One of the Wealth Insanity Cycle at maximum velocity.

In interviews conducted both before and after the collapse, Bankman-Fried described his relationship to money using language that tracks almost precisely with the dopamine research. The accumulation was never about the money itself; it was about what accumulating more of it meant about him, about his judgment, about his place in a hierarchy of minds he was perpetually trying to dominate. The effective altruism framing ('I'm doing this to give it all away') was the moral credential that allowed the escalation to continue without internal resistance. Each successful trade was a signal. Each billion was confirmation. The feedback loop had been running so long and at such intensity that the question of whether any of it was real, whether the numbers on the screen corresponded to anything in the actual world, had stopped being a constraint.

Bankman-Fried is not unusual in this regard. He is just unusually documented. The traders, founders, and executives who describe their relationship to financial success using the language of compulsion, of never-enough, of the hollow feeling that follows each new milestone; the research literature is full of their accounts. The difference between SBF and the next hundred people with the same psychological profile is not the psychology. It is whether the architecture around them failed in ways that made the fraud visible.

The money was never the point. The accumulation was the point. And the accumulation, like any other compulsive behavior, required escalation to maintain the feeling it was originally producing.

"The richest man in the room isn't the happiest. He's the most addicted."

This is not rhetorical framing. The neural pathways activated by financial reward and the neural pathways activated by cocaine are the same pathways. The mesolimbic dopamine system doesn't distinguish between snorting something in a club bathroom and closing a leveraged buyout. Both trigger the same cascade. Both create the same craving for more. Both produce a progressively desensitized reward system that demands escalating input to achieve the same neurochemical response.

This is why billionaires don't stop at $100 million. It's not greed in the simple moral sense; it's neurological addiction. The brain has been trained over years of accumulation to treat financial pursuit as a primary survival behavior, routing dopamine responses that were originally designed for food and reproduction toward the accumulation of capital. The compulsion loop is fully engaged, and unlike other addictions, this one is celebrated at fundraising dinners and profiled in Forbes.

What makes this particularly interesting, and particularly relevant to Brad, is what happens to the rest of the brain's functions as this loop deepens.

The Empathy Eviction: What Power Does to Mirror Neurons

In 2013, a neuroscientist named Sukhvinder Obhi at Wilfrid Laurier University in Ontario (later McMaster University) published research that should have been front-page news everywhere but mostly wasn't, because it didn't involve a celebrity, a scandal, or a diet. It involved transcranial magnetic stimulation machines and rubber balls, which is arguably less clickable but considerably more important.

Here's what Obhi and his colleagues found. When humans observe other people doing things (picking up a cup, squeezing a ball, shaking a hand), a network of brain regions activates in the observer that mirrors the activity they're watching. These mirror neuron networks are the neurological foundation of empathy. They're how we understand other people's actions, infer their intentions, and feel something resembling their experience. When you wince watching someone stub their toe, that's your mirror system doing exactly what it evolved to do.

Obhi's research asked a simple, devastating question: what happens to the mirror system when you give someone power?

The answer, demonstrated with the elegant brutality of controlled science, is: it shuts down.

Participants in the study were divided into groups and "primed" for high power or low power, asked to write about a time they felt powerful (high power group) or a time someone had power over them (low power group). Then they watched videos of someone squeezing a rubber ball while Obhi measured their brain's resonance, the degree to which the observer's motor cortex mirrored what they were watching.

High-power participants showed significantly reduced mirroring compared to low-power participants. The neural mechanism of empathy was measurably suppressed, not by some extraordinary intervention, but simply by priming people to feel powerful. These weren't even actually powerful people. They were college students who had spent fifteen minutes writing an essay. And their brains were already behaving differently.

Obhi described this as a kind of anesthesia of the mirror system. Not broken; anesthetized. The capacity for empathy was still structurally present. It was just switched off by the experience of power.

"Power doesn't just change what you do. It changes how your brain processes other people's existence."

His colleague Dacher Keltner at the University of California Berkeley had been arriving at the same conclusion from a behavioral direction. Keltner, who has spent more than twenty years studying the psychology of power, documented what he calls the "power paradox": the qualities that help people gain power (empathy, social attunement, listening, cooperation) are precisely the qualities that power then systematically erodes.

Keltner's research found that when people feel powerful, they judge others' emotions less accurately, listen less carefully, struggle to take other people's perspectives, and stop showing recognizable signs of compassion. In one study, participants who felt powerful, while listening to someone describe a serious personal problem (illness of a family member, workplace crisis), made less eye contact, oriented their bodies away, and engaged in what any therapist would immediately clock as active disengagement.

The kicker from a 2011 UC Berkeley study led by psychologist Jennifer Stellar, a researcher in Keltner's orbit, was particularly pointed: participants from upper-middle and upper-class backgrounds were measurably less able to feel empathy and compassion for people in distress than their lower-income counterparts. Not less willing; less able. The capacity itself was diminished.

"When we don't have power and we want to contribute, we really think carefully about other people, we listen and we adapt our behavior to the social group," Keltner has explained. "But once we have power, our focus shifts to 'What do I want?' We become focused on our desires, and that focus produces a state of mania."

A state of mania. From a Berkeley professor. About rich people. Take a moment with that.

Candy, Cars, and the Science of Not Giving a Damn

If you want hard behavioral data, not brain scans, not priming experiments, but actual observable behavior in the real world, look no further than the work of psychologist Paul Piff, who spent the better part of two years hiding in bushes near the Berkeley Marina watching fancy cars be terrible.

We're not editorializing. That is literally what happened.

Piff and his UC Berkeley colleagues set up observation posts at four-way intersections and pedestrian crosswalks and systematically watched to see whether drivers of expensive vehicles behaved differently than drivers of modest ones. The answer, published in 2012 in the Proceedings of the National Academy of Sciences, was a fairly comprehensive indictment of BMW ownership: upper-class drivers (as determined by the status of their vehicle) were four times more likely to cut off other drivers at the intersection and three times more likely to cut off pedestrians who were already in the crosswalk.

Subsequent controlled studies in the same research program were even more direct. In candy experiments, participants were told that a jar of sweets was reserved for children in a nearby lab, and that they could take some if they wanted. Wealthier participants took significantly more candy, candy intended for children, than their less wealthy peers. In negotiation experiments, upper-class participants were more likely to lie. In gaming scenarios, they were more likely to cheat to improve their odds of winning a prize. Across seven separate studies with more than 1,000 participants, the consistent finding was: higher socioeconomic status correlated with more unethical behavior.

Piff's explanation for the pattern was not that wealthy people are born without morals. It's that "the increased want associated with greater wealth and status can promote wrongdoing," and that upper-class individuals are more likely to have been exposed to cultural and economic frameworks that "moralize greed", framing self-interested behavior as rational, justified, and even admirable.

In other words: it's not just the brain chemistry. It's also the story they've been told about what the brain chemistry means.

The most alarming finding in Piff's research, and the one that should give everyone pause, is this: in the final portion of the study, when lower-class participants were encouraged to think about the positive aspects of greed, they became just as likely as their wealthy counterparts to engage in unethical behavior. The ethical lapse wasn't permanent, innate character. It was trainable. Greed, it turns out, is a learnable attitude, and wealth provides a very effective classroom.

The Cookie Monster Problem: When Powerful People Lose Self-Regulation

There's a classic Keltner anecdote that deserves to live forever in the literature of wealth psychology. In a famous experiment at Berkeley, participants were placed in a group and one person was randomly assigned authority over the others. A plate of cookies was placed on the table, four cookies for three people, so there was always a leftover. The person assigned power almost invariably took the extra cookie. More than that: they ate it in a specific way. With their mouth open. Making noise. Dropping crumbs on themselves and the table. Completely oblivious to how they appeared to others.

Keltner calls this the Cookie Monster effect. When people feel powerful, not only do they take more; they become less conscious of, and less interested in, how they come across. Social self-regulation weakens. The internal editor that makes the rest of us chew with our mouths closed and not take the last cookie at a work meeting gets quieter and quieter the higher up the ladder someone goes.

This isn't a minor quirk. The same mechanism that lets someone eat cookies obnoxiously in a lab setting is the one that lets a CEO humiliate an employee in a meeting, a billionaire dispose of an inconvenient person, or a powerful man decide that certain rules simply don't apply to him. The self-regulatory circuitry (particularly in the prefrontal cortex, which handles impulse control, consequence evaluation, and social norm adherence) is progressively overridden by the experience of power.

The research on this is consistent and longitudinal: when people feel powerful, they are more likely to make risky choices and gambles, more likely to speak their mind without filtering, more likely to physically touch others in potentially inappropriate ways, and more likely to act on their desires without the normal social friction of consequence-consideration. Keltner described this combination as resembling what you would observe in someone with damage to the brain's empathy network through head trauma.

Let that land. Head trauma. A Berkeley professor who has spent twenty years studying power is using "resembles a traumatic brain injury" as a clinical descriptor for how power affects behavior. Not as hyperbole. As science.

The Tolerance Problem: Why They Can Never Stop

Back to the dopamine loop, because it has a second act that's equally grim.

In addiction research, tolerance is the phenomenon where repeated exposure to a stimulus that generates dopamine release produces progressively diminished responses. The brain adapts. What used to create a significant neurochemical reaction starts requiring more and more input to achieve the same effect. Drug users know this well: the first hit of heroin is supposedly transcendent; the hundredth is barely keeping withdrawal at bay.

The same mechanism operates with wealth-as-reward. There is significant evidence from behavioral economics and neuroscience that the relationship between income and happiness is real, but heavily front-loaded. Research published by economists Angus Deaton and Daniel Kahneman famously found that emotional well-being increases with income, but the gains flatten substantially around $75,000 annually (a figure that has been updated in more recent research by Matthew Killingsworth at the University of Pennsylvania, who found continued, though diminishing, returns further up the income scale). The point is that the dopamine response to financial gain has a strongly diminishing return curve, but the wanting system doesn't know that.

The wanting system just knows: more produced reward before. Seek more. This creates a behavioral pattern that looks, from the outside, exactly like addiction: escalating pursuit, inability to stop, progressive disconnection from the activities and relationships that used to produce satisfaction, and a narrowing of focus onto the one behavior that still generates the reward signal, however faintly.

This is why the ultra-wealthy don't retire. It's why people with more money than they could spend in multiple lifetimes are still waking up at 5am to squeeze more out of the world. It's not ambition in the admirable sense. It's neurological compulsion. The dopamine loop has fully colonized the prefrontal cortex's goal-setting architecture, and "enough" has simply been deleted from the vocabulary of available states.

And while they're running on that loop, pursuing, acquiring, escalating, the empathy system is offline, the self-regulation is degraded, the mirror neurons are anesthetized, and the ethical frameworks are increasingly subordinated to the ideology of self-interest.

This is not a moral failing. It's a neurological sequence. Which is, depending on your perspective, either deeply reassuring or significantly more terrifying.

But Wait: Aren't Some Rich People Fine?

This is the moment where intellectual honesty requires a tap on the brakes, because the research does not say: all wealthy people are broken automatons of greed and brain damage. It doesn't work that way.

What the research says is: these are statistically significant patterns that become more pronounced with greater wealth accumulation and longer duration of power. They are tendencies, not certainties. Effect sizes, not destiny. Piff himself is careful to note exceptions; the notably generous philanthropy of certain ultra-wealthy individuals demonstrates that the neurological default effects of power and wealth can be resisted with conscious effort, structural accountability, and maintained social engagement with diverse populations.

Keltner's own framework ultimately argues that awareness of these tendencies is the first line of defense against them. If you know power anesthetizes your mirror system, you can compensate. If you know your dopamine loop is running hot, you can build structures that redirect it. The problem is that most powerful people don't know, or don't believe, or are too thoroughly surrounded by people who are financially incentivized to tell them they're doing great.

Which brings us to the most darkly comedic finding in all of this research: the very neural changes that power and wealth produce make it progressively harder to recognize those neural changes in yourself. The decreased perspective-taking, the reduced social attunement, the weakened self-regulatory function. These are exactly the capacities you would need to notice that your brain is behaving differently. Power doesn't just change you. It makes you less able to see that you've changed.

The system is airtight.

And Brad, standing in his Aspen chalet with his NDA and his helicopter pad, has absolutely no idea what happened to him.

That's the point of this book. You will.

Brad's brain didn't betray him randomly. It followed a documented sequence, one that starts with reward circuitry and ends somewhere considerably darker. Stage One of the Wealth Insanity Cycle is now accounted for. The dopamine system has been captured. Next, we look at what power does to the brain after the money has already done its work.

Chapter 2

Power Poisoning

How Authority Literally Brain-Damages People

Lead paint. Mercury. Power. All neurotoxins. Two of them are banned.

The third one runs most of the world's major institutions.

There is a specific category of congressional hearing that political scientists have studied for decades: the accountability hearing. A powerful executive sits before elected representatives and explains, under oath, what happened on their watch. The hearings follow a predictable structure: prepared statements, pointed questions, careful lawyerly deflection. Most executives are good at it. They've been briefed. They know the choreography.

What researchers who study these hearings have noticed is not the deflection. That's expected. What's interesting is the other thing: the executives who appear not to be deflecting at all, who seem to have genuinely lost the cognitive architecture required to understand what the senators are asking. Not because they're hiding something. Because the capacity to process other people's reality has, over years of accumulated power, quietly gone offline.

John Stumpf arrived at his congressional hearing in September 2016 as the CEO of Wells Fargo, one of the largest banks in the United States. He had been with the company for thirty-four years. He was, by every conventional metric, at the absolute pinnacle of American financial power.

He was there to explain why his bank had opened approximately two million fraudulent accounts, accounts that real customers never requested, never wanted, and in many cases didn't discover until mysterious fees began appearing and collection agencies began calling. The scheme had run for years, driven by an internal sales culture that set quotas so aggressive that employees opened fake accounts to meet them, then scrambled to prevent customers from noticing.

Stumpf sat before Congress and could not explain what happened. Not in the lawyerly, self-protective way of a man being careful not to incriminate himself. In a genuinely appears-to-have-lost-the-capacity-to-process-other-people's-reality way. He deflected. He repeated talking points. He expressed vague sorrow about outcomes without registering anything resembling comprehension of actual human harm. Senators from both parties were visibly incredulous. Senator Elizabeth Warren told him he should resign. He looked like a man who had been asked to explain a foreign concept for which he had no native vocabulary.

He resigned six weeks later.

What happened to John Stumpf is not a mystery, not to neuroscientists and behavioral researchers who have been studying exactly this phenomenon for decades. What happened to Stumpf is what happens to a lot of people who hold significant power for a significant amount of time: the power poisoned him. Gradually, thoroughly, and with the efficient brutality of any good neurotoxin.

Chapter One established that money and power change how the brain's reward circuits and mirror neuron systems operate. This chapter goes further. Here we're talking about power that has been held long enough, at sufficient magnitude, that it produces something resembling an acquired personality disorder: a documented, diagnosable, progressive deterioration of the mental capacities most essential to good leadership and decent human behavior.

There is a clinical name for this. A British neurologist-turned-politician named it. And the list of people who have had it reads like a who's who of history's most consequential disasters.

Hubris Syndrome: The Disorder Nobody's Treating

Lord David Owen is, by any measure, a man who knows his way around power. He served as a physician, became a Member of Parliament at thirty, was appointed British Foreign Secretary at thirty-eight, the youngest in a century, and co-founded a political party, and eventually became a member of the House of Lords. He has watched power operate from the inside for six decades.

He is also a trained neurologist. And in 2006, after years of observing something he couldn't find adequate clinical language for, he published a paper in the Journal of the Royal Society of Medicine proposing a new medical category: hubris syndrome.

In 2009, Owen partnered with Jonathan Davidson, a professor of psychiatry and behavioral sciences at Duke University Medical Center, to publish a landmark paper in Brain, one of the most prestigious journals in neuroscience, formally mapping what they called "an acquired personality disorder." Unlike most personality disorders, which appear in early adulthood and are relatively stable, hubris syndrome emerges after power has been held for a sustained period and largely resolves when the power is removed. It is, in Owen's framing, a disorder of the possession of power, specifically power associated with overwhelming success, held for years, with minimal external constraint.

Owen and Davidson identified fourteen clinical symptoms of the syndrome and proposed that a diagnosis requires at least three, including at least one of five unique criteria. Let's walk through the ones that will be familiar to anyone who has spent time watching extraordinarily wealthy or powerful people operate:

Lord David Owen, when developing the clinical criteria for hubris syndrome, did not need to invent examples. He had a filing cabinet full of them. Enron is among the most legible.

At its peak in 2000, Enron was the seventh-largest company in the United States by revenue, employing approximately 29,000 people and reporting revenues of $111 billion. Its CEO, Jeffrey Skilling, was celebrated as a visionary, a man who had transformed a natural gas pipeline company into what he described as 'the world's greatest company.' Fortune named Enron the most innovative company in America for six consecutive years. The stock price had increased 89 percent in 2000 alone.

The company was also, beneath the reported numbers, largely fictional. Enron's profitability depended on a set of accounting practices, mark-to-market valuation of speculative future contracts, the use of off-balance-sheet partnerships to hide debt, and the systematic inflation of projected revenues, all of which required sustained institutional collusion to maintain. When the structure collapsed in late 2001, approximately $74 billion in shareholder value was destroyed. Thousands of employees lost their retirement savings. Skilling was convicted of fraud and conspiracy. Enron's accounting firm, Arthur Andersen, collapsed entirely.

What makes Enron specifically illustrative for this chapter is not the fraud mechanism (accounting fraud is old and well-documented). It is the internal culture that the Owen-Davidson criteria describe almost perfectly. Former employees' accounts of Enron's executive culture are consistent across dozens of journalistic and legal records: a contempt for those who questioned the numbers that 'bordered on disdain.' An identification of Skilling's personal vision with the company's mission so complete that challenging one was tantamount to attacking the other. An unshakeable belief in personal judgment combined with a systematic refusal to take advice from anyone who was not already a true believer. A loss of contact with financial reality that was, by the end, organizational rather than merely individual;

the entire executive suite had inhabited the fictional version of the company for long enough that the gap between the story and the numbers had ceased to register as a problem.

Owen's diagnostic framework requires three symptoms, including at least one unique criterion. Enron's C-suite, by the time of the collapse, was presenting something closer to the full fourteen. The board of directors, which had suspended its own ethics policy to allow the off-balance-sheet structures, had been recruited into the syndrome. The auditors, who had abandoned their professional obligations to maintain the relationship, had been recruited into it. The financial analysts, who continued issuing buy recommendations on a company whose numbers made no mathematical sense, had been recruited into it. Hubris syndrome, at sufficient institutional scale, becomes contagious.

The lesson that Enron offered, and that the subsequent decades of corporate scandal have not dislodged, is that the syndrome is not stopped by intelligence, credentials, or proximity to the evidence. Every person in that building was smart enough to know what they were looking at. That was not sufficient.

A messianic way of talking and a tendency toward grandiosity in speech and manner. An identification with the organization or nation so complete that the person's interests and the institution's interests are perceived as identical. A contempt for others bordering on disdain. An unshakeable belief in personal judgment, combined with a refusal to take advice. A loss of contact with reality. Recklessness to the point of incompetence. An obsession with image. And, notably, a tendency to refer to themselves in the third person, or to use the royal 'we.'

Margaret Thatcher famously announced, after the birth of her grandchild: 'We have become a grandmother.' Tony Blair's trajectory, from the empathetic, listening candidate of 1997 to the hyperactive, messianic co-architect of the Iraq War, is considered by Owen one of the clearest modern case studies of the syndrome in action. George W. Bush's 'Mission Accomplished' aircraft carrier moment was identified as the peak expression of his own case. Owen counted five definite cases among the fourteen US Presidents and UK Prime Ministers who served over the period he studied.

"Power is as potent a brain-changer as any drug. And some people simply do not have the rooted character necessary to counteract it." — Lord David Owen

Owen is careful to note what this is and isn't. Hubris syndrome is not a pre-existing mental illness. It is not bipolar disorder, narcissistic personality disorder, or antisocial personality disorder, though it shares surface features with all three and must be clinically distinguished from them. It is an acquired condition, meaning it develops after exposure to the specific environment of significant power. It can affect people with no prior psychological history. It is, in that sense, an environmental disease, as predictable as mesothelioma in asbestos workers or coal miner's lung.

The environment is power. The disease is hubris syndrome. And your boss has probably had a low-grade version of it for years.

The Five Stages of Going Completely Off the Rails

Before Owen gave it a clinical name, organizational researchers were already documenting the same progression through a different lens. In 1991, Donald Hambrick and Richard Fukutomi published a model in Administrative Science Quarterly describing what they called the "seasons" of a CEO's tenure: a five-stage lifecycle of executive behavior that, in its final phase, arrives at a place they clinically termed dysfunction.

The model goes like this. In the early stages, a new CEO is appropriately humble. They're gathering information from diverse sources, adapting their leadership to the specific environment, and staying closely attuned to feedback because they're still earning legitimacy. They know they don't know everything. This humility is not a character virtue; it's a rational response to insufficient information. They need input because they haven't yet formed fixed opinions about what's correct.

Over time, typically across years, successful CEOs develop what the researchers called commitment to a paradigm. Their accumulated experience becomes a framework through which they interpret new information. This is initially a feature, not a bug. Pattern recognition is valuable. Experience produces efficiency.

But the process doesn't stop there. As the tenure extends, the successful paradigm becomes a filter that increasingly excludes information that doesn't confirm it. The sources of input narrow. The tolerance for dissent decreases. The internal conviction that one's own judgment is reliable, a conviction that has been rewarded repeatedly by success, becomes progressively less correctable by external reality.

In the final phase of long tenure, Hambrick and Fukutomi identified what they called increasing cognitive rigidity. The CEO's model of the world has essentially calcified. They are no longer processing new information so much as confirming existing conclusions. Research on CEO tenure and firm performance published in the Harvard Business Review confirms what the model predicts: CEOs tend to be most effective in their early years, with performance peaking roughly in the middle of tenure and then declining, sometimes sharply, as they move into the later stages of cognitive entrenchment.

In a sample of firms in the semiconductor industry, researcher Warren Boeker found a clear negative linear relationship between CEO tenure length and the organization's capacity for strategic change. The longer the CEO, the more rigid the strategy. The more rigid the strategy, the less the organization could adapt. Eventually, the CEO's worldview became the organization's ceiling.

This is what cognitive calcification looks like from the outside: a powerful person who was once visionary becoming increasingly convinced that the same approaches that worked before will continue to work, who interprets declining results as temporary external factors rather than evidence of a need for change, and who progressively eliminates from their circle anyone who might suggest otherwise.

Enter the yes-men.

The Yes-Man Ecosystem: How Power Builds Its Own Insulation

Here is one of the great structural ironies of organizational life: the higher someone rises, the less likely they are to receive honest information, and the more they need it.

The reasons are not mysterious. People who work for powerful individuals are, by definition, in a position of financial and professional dependency. Their livelihoods are contingent on the goodwill of the person above them. And human beings, as a species, have a well-documented tendency to tell people with power what those people want to hear. Socrates was cataloguing this problem around 400 B.C. It is not a new discovery. It is a feature of social hierarchies that has operated consistently across every culture and era for which we have records.

What researchers have documented more recently is how the powerful person's own psychology actively accelerates this dynamic. Remember from Chapter One that power suppresses the mirror neuron system and reduces perspective-taking capacity. A CEO who has been in their role for eight years is both less capable of reading accurate emotional feedback from others AND surrounded by people who have been financially conditioned to provide inaccurate emotional feedback. The distortion compounds from both directions simultaneously.

Irving Janis, a Yale psychologist, coined the term groupthink in 1972 to describe the phenomenon where groups in high-stakes situations prioritize internal harmony and consensus over critical thinking, producing what Janis called a deterioration of mental efficiency, reality testing, and moral judgment. Janis used the term to explain catastrophic collective decisions including the Bay of Pigs invasion and the failure to anticipate the attack on Pearl Harbor. But groupthink is not just a risk in high-stakes government situations. It is the default operating mode of any organization where the person at the top has sufficient power to reward agreement and punish dissent, whether explicitly or simply through the social physics of hierarchy.

“Remember that the higher you are, the more likely you are to be ingratiated. Get advice from people who do not depend on you.” — Ithai Stern, organizational researcher

The practical consequence: a long-tenured, powerful person, whether in government, finance, or industry, is operating on a progressively less accurate map of reality. They receive filtered information from people motivated to please them. They process that filtered information through a cognitive framework that has become increasingly resistant to revision. They are surrounded by organizational structures they created, which were built around their own preferences and blind spots. And they have neurologically reduced capacity for the empathy, perspective-taking, and self-awareness that might otherwise allow them to notice this happening.

It is, in systems terms, a perfectly closed feedback loop. And it is running in the direction of disaster.

Hubris Syndrome in the Boardroom: Not Just a Government Problem

Owen is explicit on this point: hubris syndrome is not exclusive to heads of state. He notes specifically that the 2008 global financial collapse was accompanied by clear evidence of the syndrome among leading international bankers. The extraordinary leverage, the disregard for risk modeling that contradicted established assumptions, the near-universal failure among senior financial leaders to register the systemic dangers being flagged by analysts. This is not what careful, reality-testing minds look like. This is what cognitively calcified, hubris-affected minds look like.

The CEO overconfidence research supports this clinical observation with hard data. A study examining US firm data from 1996 to 2014, published in the Journal of Business Research, found that CEO power is a significant predictor of CEO overconfidence, measured through behavioral indicators like holding stock options far past rational exercise thresholds. Powerful CEOs overestimate the future performance of their companies in ways that have measurable financial consequences for everyone who depends on those companies.

The "blind power" research from that study describes an elegant and miserable dynamic: the CEO's power leads to overconfidence, the overconfidence produces poor decision-making, and the organizational power the CEO commands means that poor decision-making proceeds largely unchallenged until the consequences become impossible to deny. By which point, significant damage has already been done.

Think of the examples that practically write themselves: the telecommunications executive who dismissed mobile internet as a fad, the retail CEO who declared e-commerce a passing trend while competitors were building supply chains, the financial institution leader who told regulators that the mortgage instruments his firm was creating were sound because his team was the best in the business. In each case: a long-tenured leader, an insulated environment, a calcified paradigm, a shortage of dissent, and a spectacular collision with reality.

Owen identifies a particularly telling behavioral marker of advanced hubris syndrome that appears consistently across cases: the leader stops distinguishing between themselves and the institution they run. The CEO of the company begins to believe that what is good for them personally is definitionally good for the company. The head of state starts to treat national interests as an extension of personal interests. This merger of self and institution produces decisions that serve the individual while being catastrophically explained as serving the collective, and the individual genuinely cannot see the distinction.

This is not cynical manipulation. That would actually require a functional theory of mind, an ability to model what others are thinking and strategically deceive them. Hubris syndrome, at its advanced stages, has eliminated the capacity for that kind of meta-cognition. The person isn't lying about serving the institution. They've lost the ability to distinguish the two.

The Reversibility Question: Is Any of This Fixable?

Here is the part that is either hopeful or deeply frustrating, depending on your relationship to the people in question.

Owen's clinical observation, supported by his review of historical cases, is that hubris syndrome typically remits when the person leaves power. The symptoms abate. The grandiosity subsides. The reality-testing improves. Margaret Thatcher, after her removal from office, reportedly became markedly more reflective and less certain than she had been in her final years in power. Tony Blair's post-office behavior and statements have shown more nuance than his in-office persona, though Owen would argue the damage done during the hubristic period was not reversed by its resolution.

This reversibility is, in a strange way, part of what distinguishes hubris syndrome from a permanent personality disorder. It is not who these people are. It is what power did to them. Remove the environmental condition, and the worst of the symptoms fade. Which is simultaneously reassuring (people are not inevitably broken) and infuriating (the harm they caused while broken doesn't disappear with their recovery).

Owen and Davidson are also specific about the factors that make some people more resistant to hubris syndrome than others: retained personal modesty while in power, maintained engagement with people outside one's immediate circle, a functional sense of humor and capacity for self-deprecation, genuine openness to criticism, and what they call an ability to be laughed at. These are not complicated qualities. They are, in fact, the qualities most directly targeted and eroded by the environment of power itself.

Which brings us back to the structural problem that will recur throughout this book. The syndrome is treatable if you can maintain access to the conditions that prevent it. But the experience of power progressively destroys your access to those conditions. Humility becomes harder as success compounds. Honest criticism becomes rarer as dependency deepens. The very qualities Owen identifies as protective are the qualities power erodes most efficiently.

Hambrick and Fukutomi's five-stage model ends in dysfunction. Owen's fourteen-symptom clinical picture ends in what he calls hubristic incompetence. The CEO overconfidence research ends in catastrophic strategic failures and organizations that underperform long after the hubris-affected leader has finally been removed.

And through all of it, the people at the top, the ones with the most resources, the most decision-making power, and the most capacity to do harm or good at scale, are the least likely to have an accurate perception of their own cognitive state.

John Stumpf thought he was a great leader until Congress showed him otherwise. And he probably wasn't entirely wrong; he had been, at some point. It's just that somewhere in the previous decade of unchallenged power, the person who had been a great leader had slowly, quietly, and completely left the building.

The building was still standing. The lights were still on. The press releases still called him visionary.

Nobody had told him he'd become the building.

John Stumpf sat before Congress and could not access the cognitive machinery required to understand what he had done. That machinery had been degraded, over decades of accumulated power, in a measurable and predictable way. Stage Two of the Cycle, Power Poisoning, is the neurological process that turns the reward-chasing of Stage One into something more structurally dangerous: a person at the top of a major institution who is no longer reliably able to perceive the humans below them. Stage Three is about where those people tend to end up.

Chapter 3

Psychopaths in Suits

The Corporate Ladder as Screening Tool

Not all psychopaths are in prison. Some of them are running your quarterly performance review.

In 2004, a researcher named Paul Babiak was helping a Fortune 500 company assess its senior leadership pipeline. This was routine consulting work: personality assessments, structured interviews, the kind of evaluation that large companies pay for when they want to identify high-potential talent before promoting them. Babiak had done hundreds of these.

About forty minutes into one particular interview, he stopped writing.

The executive across from him was impressive. Charismatic. Fluent. He had a way of making the conversation feel like a collaboration, as if the two of them were solving something together. His answers were perfectly calibrated: confident without arrogance, self-aware without vulnerability. He mentioned his team constantly, always with warmth. He described his management philosophy in terms of service and development. He was exactly what the company had asked Babiak to find.

Babiak had also, earlier that week, interviewed three of this man's direct reports. Quietly. Separately. Confidentially.

Every single one of them had described, in their own language and with varying degrees of hesitation, the same person. Someone who took credit for others' work without acknowledgment. Who isolated employees from each other so that no one could compare notes. Who delivered criticism in front of witnesses and praise in private, ensuring the public record favored his narrative. Who, when confronted about any of this, responded with a version of events so plausible and so detailed that the person raising the concern often ended the meeting wondering if they had misremembered.

Babiak recognized the pattern. He had seen it before, in a very different professional context.

He was a psychologist who had spent years studying psychopathy. Not the cinematic version with the ominous music and the basement. The clinical version: the constellation of traits that includes superficial charm, pathological manipulation, absence of genuine empathy, and a capacity for harm that is entirely unbothered by guilt or remorse. He had studied these traits in prisons. Now he was watching them perform flawlessly in a corner office.

He wasn't the only one who had noticed. A year earlier, in 2003, researchers Belinda Board and Katarina Fritzon at the University of Surrey had published findings that should have made considerably more headlines than they did. They had taken a group of senior British business executives and given them the same psychological assessment used at Broadmoor Hospital, one of Britain's highest-security psychiatric facilities, housing offenders society has determined cannot safely exist outside a locked institution.

The executives scored higher than the Broadmoor patients on three categories: histrionic personality disorder, narcissistic personality disorder, and compulsive personality disorder. Not slightly higher. Statistically, measurably, significantly higher. Board and Fritzon coined a term for what they found: 'successful psychopaths.' The Broadmoor patients, by contrast, were 'unsuccessful psychopaths.' The distinction between the two groups was not the presence or absence of psychopathic traits. It was whether those traits had produced a corner office or a criminal conviction.

This chapter is about why that distinction exists, and why the system keeps producing it.

Because, as it turns out, they don't.

What Psychopathy Actually Is (And Isn't)

Let's get the Hannibal Lecter out of the room right now.

Popular culture has a psychopath problem. Not a shortage of them; a misrepresentation of them. The cinematic psychopath is brilliant, theatrical, violent, and impossible to miss. He monologues. He wears restraints. He has unsettling taste in classical music and an interest in the interior of skulls. This portrait is useful for screenwriters and almost completely useless for understanding the actual phenomenon.

Real psychopathy, as assessed clinically using Robert Hare's Psychopathy Checklist-Revised (PCL-

R), the gold standard diagnostic instrument developed over decades and validated across thousands of studies, is a constellation of traits organized around two core clusters. The first cluster involves interpersonal and affective features: glibness, superficial charm, grandiose self-worth, pathological lying, conning and manipulativeness, shallow emotional affect, lack of remorse or guilt, and callousness toward others. The second cluster involves antisocial behaviors: impulsivity, poor behavioral controls, early behavioral problems, juvenile delinquency, revocation of conditional release, and a generally parasitic lifestyle.

What makes the corporate version interesting, and what Board and Fritzon's research specifically illuminated, is that the first cluster, the interpersonal and affective features, can exist in full clinical force without the second. The charm, the manipulation, the absence of genuine empathy, the grandiosity, the pathological self-focus: these can all be present without the impulsivity and behavioral dyscontrol that typically leads people into prisons. The corporate psychopath has everything that makes psychopathy dangerous, with just enough executive function to keep it inside the law.

Robert Hare, who literally wrote the book on psychopathy (and then wrote several more), has given presentations to law enforcement and corporate audiences using a version of the same line: not all psychopaths are in prison. Some are in the boardroom. He does not say this to be provocative. He says it because the data backs him up.

"Not all psychopaths are in prison. Some are in the boardroom." — Robert D. Hare, Ph.D., creator of the Psychopathy Checklist-Revised

Psychopathy is also, crucially, a spectrum. You do not flip from 'normal person' to 'psychopath' at a single threshold; you exist somewhere on a continuum of traits. Subclinical psychopathy (what researchers increasingly call 'corporate psychopathy') describes individuals who score meaningfully higher than the general population on the interpersonal and affective dimensions of the scale without reaching clinical thresholds for diagnosis or displaying the kind of overt antisocial behavior that draws legal consequences. These people are among us. Some of them are running meetings you attend on a regular basis.

The Numbers: How Many Psychopaths Are Actually Up There?

In the general population, full-threshold psychopathy occurs at roughly 1% prevalence. One in a hundred people. Not trivial; that means at any given time there are approximately 80 million psychopaths globally, but low enough that you can go through a lot of ordinary life without knowingly encountering one.

Then Paul Babiak and Robert Hare ran their study.

In 2010, Babiak, Neumann, and Hare published results from an examination of 203 high-potential corporate professionals, people selected by their companies to participate in management development programs. These were not random employees. They were the chosen ones: vice presidents, supervisors, directors, the people their organizations had identified as having senior leadership potential. The researchers administered the PCL-R and compared results against community samples.

The rate of psychopathic traits in this corporate cohort was 3.9%. Nearly four times the general population prevalence. And this was in a sample specifically selected for high potential, meaning the more power someone had accumulated or was being groomed to accumulate, the more likely they were to show psychopathic scoring.

The findings were worse on closer examination. Among those who scored highest on the PCL-R, in-house performance ratings showed a revealing pattern. High-psychopathy executives received elevated ratings on charisma and presentation style; they were seen as creative, strong strategic thinkers, excellent communicators. They received lower ratings on responsibility and performance: being a team player, actual management quality, and overall accomplishments. In other words: they looked spectacular in meetings and in front of cameras. They were demonstrably worse at actually running things.

They had been selected, rewarded, and promoted on the basis of exactly the wrong criteria.

The 2005 Dutton Great British Psychopath Survey, conducted at Oxford, produced a list of the ten professions with the highest proportion of psychopathic traits. The top spot went to CEO.

Number two was lawyer. Number three was media personality. The list reads, with modest adjustments for geography and era, like a roster of people who run most of the institutions that shape your daily life.

Kevin Dutton, the Oxford psychologist who compiled the survey and wrote The Wisdom of Psychopaths, puts the mechanism bluntly: the corporate world offers everything the psychopathic personality finds rewarding (money, power, status, control) in an environment that rewards exactly the traits psychopathy produces: fearlessness, ruthlessness, charm, and a complete absence of the anxiety that paralyzes normal people when they contemplate hurting others to get ahead.

The Hiring Problem: We Built a Psychopath-Friendly Filter

Here is the exquisitely awkward part.

We did not accidentally stumble into this situation. We selected our way into it. Corporate hiring practices, particularly at senior levels, have historically screened for characteristics that overlap substantially with the charming, confident, high-functioning face of subclinical psychopathy.

Consider what the standard executive hiring process rewards. Confidence bordering on certainty. Compelling narrative construction about one's accomplishments. Smooth, authoritative performance under pressure. The ability to read a room and tell people what they want to hear. Decisiveness presented as vision. Emotional control presented as stability. A compelling external presentation maintained regardless of what is actually happening internally.

These are, literally, skills that psychopaths are structurally better at than normal people, not because they practice them harder, but because the internal experience that makes these behaviors costly for non-psychopaths is simply absent for them. A non-psychopathic executive who claims credit for colleagues' work feels guilt. A psychopathic one doesn't. A non-psychopathic executive performing confidence in a collapsing situation experiences cortisol-spiking stress that leaks into their presentation. A psychopathic one experiences it as an interesting problem to manage. A non-psychopathic executive who has to fire hundreds of people to protect quarterly numbers loses sleep. A psychopathic one schedules the call and goes to dinner.

The hiring filter does not see the absence of internal experience. It sees the output: smooth, confident, compelling performance. It concludes: leadership material. It promotes accordingly.

Babiak and Hare describe the corporate psychopath's climb to power as a five-stage operation. Entry: using highly developed social skills and charm to obtain the position. Assessment: identifying useful pawns and patrons, who has informal influence, who has formal power, and who can be manipulated. Manipulation: constructing what they call a psychopathic fiction, circulating positive information about themselves while systematically undermining competitors. Confrontation: when exposed, responding with aggression, denial, and counter-attack. Ascension:

reaching the position of power and discarding anyone who helped get there.

This is not a rare career trajectory. It is, Babiak and Hare argue, documented repeatedly across industries and organizational sizes. The pattern is consistent enough that they built an assessment tool specifically designed to detect it in organizational settings, the B-Scan 360, because the standard interview process doesn't just fail to catch it. It actively rewards it.

Board and Fritzon described successful executives as 'successful psychopaths' and the Broadmoor patients as 'unsuccessful psychopaths.' The difference between the two groups was not the traits. It was the suit.

What Corporate Psychopaths Actually Do to Organizations

At this point, some well-meaning reader, perhaps one who has read enough about evolutionary psychology to have developed a reflexive contrarianism toward anything that sounds like it might be critical of high achievers, might be formulating an objection. Don't these traits help organizations? Isn't ruthless decisiveness exactly what you need at the top? Isn't the capacity to make hard calls without emotional interference precisely what separates great leaders from mediocre ones?

This argument has been made. Kevin Dutton, in The Wisdom of Psychopaths, gives it a fair hearing and finds genuine cases where specific psychopathic traits (coolness under pressure, fearlessness, ability to act decisively in crisis) produce outcomes that benefit others. There are surgeons who are better at their jobs because they can emotionally detach from patient distress during operations. There are Special Forces soldiers whose reduced fear response makes them more effective in genuinely dangerous situations. Dutton is careful to note these are highly context-specific, trait-specific observations that require significant moderating conditions to produce good outcomes.

What the organizational research shows is that in corporate environments, the context we actually care about for this chapter, the net effect of psychopathic leadership is clearly, consistently negative. Not ambiguous. Not a mixed bag requiring careful nuance. Negative.

In Full

Robert Hare's Psychopathy Checklist-Revised was not designed as a business leadership assessment. But if you applied it to the public record of Elizabeth Holmes's conduct as founder and CEO of Theranos, item by item, the exercise becomes uncomfortable in a very specific way.

Holmes founded Theranos in 2003 at nineteen, claiming the company's technology could run hundreds of diagnostic tests from a single finger-prick of blood. The claim was false. The technology did not work. Holmes knew it did not work, or had access to information that would have made this clear to any reasonably attentive person, for most of the company's existence. She raised approximately $945 million from investors, recruited a board of distinguished former government officials and executives, ran the company for more than a decade, and during that period delivered blood test results to actual patients, real medical decisions made by real people based on data generated by a machine that was producing largely unreliable output.

Holmes was convicted of fraud in 2022 and sentenced to eleven years in federal prison.

The forensic picture assembled during her trial and in subsequent journalistic accounts (John Carreyrou's Bad Blood (2018) remains the definitive account) maps to the PCL-R's first factor with a consistency that Hare himself has noted publicly is striking. Glibness and superficial charm: Holmes was uniformly described by investors, journalists, and employees as extraordinarily compelling in person, with an ability to project certainty and warmth that persisted even when the people she was charming were in possession of evidence that contradicted everything she was saying. Grandiose sense of self-worth: she compared herself explicitly and repeatedly to Steve Jobs, adopted his wardrobe as a deliberate signal, and maintained a self-narrative of world-historical importance that never meaningfully deflated despite a decade of failed technology. Pathological lying: the trial record is a catalog. Manipulativeness: she assembled a board whose prestige and connections she used as a credibility shield, cultivated a relationship with former Secretary of State George Shultz specifically for the institutional legitimacy it provided, and managed her investors' access to information with a precision that required sustained and deliberate effort. Callousness and lack of empathy: the patients whose medical decisions were affected by unreliable test results were, in every documented account of Holmes's internal deliberations, effectively absent from the calculus.

What the Theranos case illustrates specifically for this chapter is the role of institutional validation in amplifying the successful psychopath's reach. Holmes did not operate in a vacuum. She operated in an environment: Silicon Valley's 'fake it till you make it' culture, a venture capital ecosystem that rewarded confidence over evidence, a board whose members were distinguished enough to lend credibility and insufficiently technical to verify the claims, structurally optimized to reward exactly the profile she presented and structurally unable to detect what was underneath it.

The company that designed that environment did not intend to select for fraud. It selected for the behavioral profile associated with successful psychopathy (charisma, certainty, risk tolerance, vision), and fraud was, in this case, what came with it.

The board of Theranos included two former Secretaries of State, a former Secretary of Defense, and several decorated generals. None of them could do a blood test. The traits that got Holmes into that room were the same traits that made the room unable to see what she was.

Clive Boddy, a researcher at Middlesex University Business School who has spent more than a decade specifically studying corporate psychopaths and organizational outcomes, found in multiple studies that the presence of corporate psychopaths in leadership positions is associated with significantly higher rates of workplace bullying, lower employee well-being, increased organizational conflict, and reduced performance. A 2011 study by Boddy published in the Journal of Business Ethics documented that employees working under psychopathic managers reported higher levels of psychological distress and job dissatisfaction, even when controlling for other organizational factors.

The Babiak and Hare research reinforced this from the other direction: while high-psychopathy executives received elevated ratings on charisma, their actual performance metrics (team management, responsibility, objective accomplishments) were measurably lower. The impression of excellence was inversely correlated with the reality of it. They looked better than they performed. The gap between perception and reality was, in fact, one of the diagnostic indicators.

Then there are the macro-scale consequences. Owen, in his analysis of hubris syndrome, specifically noted that the 2008 global financial collapse bore clear evidence of corporate psychopathy at senior levels, the systematic dismissal of risk modeling that contradicted established assumptions, the contempt for internal dissent, the willingness to generate products designed to fail while betting against them, the ability to collect extraordinary personal compensation while the institutional damage was being distributed to people who had nothing to do with its creation. These are not the behaviors of people experiencing the normal human friction of guilt and empathy. These are the behaviors of people for whom the normal human friction of guilt and empathy is simply not running.

The Spectrum Problem and the Nuance We Owe

Let us be accurate, because accuracy matters more than a clean argument.

Psychopathy is a spectrum, and most of the research we have discussed concerns elevated traits rather than clinical diagnosis. The line between 'a person with some psychopathic traits that help them succeed in competitive environments' and 'a person who is a full-spectrum corporate psychopath causing systematic harm' is real and meaningful. The majority of senior executives, even the wealthy and the powerful, are not psychopaths in any clinically meaningful sense. Many are genuinely decent human beings who work hard and treat people fairly.

The research also has limitations that honest authors are obligated to acknowledge. The Babiak, Neumann, and Hare 2010 study had a sample of 203, useful but not enormous, and selected from a specific pool of management development candidates that may not represent the broader executive population. The Board and Fritzon findings involve a relatively small sample and a cross-sectional design that cannot establish causal mechanisms. Boddy's organizational research, while consistent, relies partly on self-report data and surveys that have the standard limitations of that methodology. The picture these studies collectively paint is credible and concerning, but it should be held with the appropriate epistemic weight rather than wielded as settled fact.

There is also the question of whether the traits associated with psychopathy in these contexts are genuinely psychopathic in nature or whether they reflect other personality profiles (narcissistic personality disorder, Machiavellianism, or simply high-functioning ambition) that share surface features without sharing the full clinical picture. The 'dark triad' (narcissism, Machiavellianism, and psychopathy) is a well-studied construct in organizational psychology precisely because these traits co-occur and interact in ways that make clean separation difficult.

What the research does establish, consistently and across multiple methodologies and research groups, is that the cluster of traits associated with subclinical psychopathy is overrepresented among people who reach the top of corporate hierarchies, and that the presence of these traits in leadership positions produces measurable negative outcomes for the organizations and people those leaders are supposed to serve. This is not a fringe finding. It is a reasonably well-supported pattern that the corporate world has been notably reluctant to incorporate into its hiring and governance practices.

The reason it hasn't been incorporated is itself worth examining. Screening for psychopathic traits in executive hiring would require organizations to actively look for the absence of certain internal experiences in candidates who have been trained their entire careers to perform those experiences convincingly. It would require prioritizing character assessment over performance metrics in a business culture that has spent forty years building ever more sophisticated performance metrics and almost no equivalent infrastructure for character evaluation. It would require boards and HR departments to acknowledge, at some level, that the people they've been selecting and promoting may have been selected and promoted partly because of psychological features that actively harm the people around them.

That is an uncomfortable thing to build into your onboarding process. And so most organizations don't.

Why This Matters Beyond the Headlines

You might be wondering why a book about wealthy people being insane is spending a full chapter on psychopathy rather than staying in the comfortable territory of the neuroscience and brain damage material from chapters one and two. The answer is that psychopathy is not a chapter addition; it is the through-line.

The three phenomena we've established across these opening chapters are not separate stories. They reinforce each other in a system. The dopamine reward circuitry that makes wealth neurologically addictive produces behavior that looks psychopathic. The mirror neuron suppression that power causes produces emotional detachment that looks psychopathic. The hubris syndrome that extended power induces (the grandiosity, the contempt, the disconnection from reality), looks psychopathic. And running underneath all of it, in some meaningful percentage of cases, is actual elevated psychopathic trait structure that arrived before the wealth and power and has been amplified by them ever since.

The corporate world has optimized for a psychological profile. That profile, it turns out, has a clinical name. The name is not flattering. The implications of having built our economic system to preferentially select for and reward this profile are, well. That's what the rest of this book is for.

Robert Hare spent his career trying to understand psychopathy in prisons. Late in that career, he turned to corporate environments and found the same thing in better offices. The suits are nicer. The damage is larger. The accountability is notably thinner.

The Broadmoor patients, at minimum, are contained.

The Broadmoor comparison is not an accident. The traits that institutional hierarchies select for and reward are the same traits the research literature associates with psychopathy, and the two populations are measurably converging at the top. Stage Three of the Cycle is not about individual monsters. It is about a filtering system that reliably produces a specific kind of leader. Stage Four examines what that leader does to the people around them over time.

Chapter 4

This Isn't New

A Brief History of Wealthy People Losing Their Minds

Rome, 70 BCE. A senator named Marcus Licinius Crassus has just finished calculating his net worth.

The number, adjusted for modern equivalents by economic historians, lands somewhere between $170 billion and $200 billion. Crassus was the wealthiest man in the Roman Republic, possibly the wealthiest man in the ancient world. He achieved this through a combination of silver mining, real estate speculation, and a fire brigade scheme so audacious it would be illegal in every jurisdiction on earth today: when a building caught fire in Rome, Crassus's private firefighters would arrive at the scene and wait. They would not begin work until Crassus himself, or one of his agents, had negotiated a purchase price for the burning building with its panicked owner. If the owner agreed, they extinguished the fire. If the owner refused, they watched it burn.

Crassus owned much of Rome's real estate. He had purchased most of it this way.

He also owned an estimated ten thousand slaves, funded political campaigns to guarantee favorable legislation, used personal wealth to equip private armies, and lobbied relentlessly against reforms that would have distributed land to Rome's landless poor. He was famously quoted saying that no man should be called rich unless he could afford to raise an army entirely from his own resources.

He was also, by the standards of his class and time, perfectly normal. Not an aberration. Not a villain in a story otherwise populated by virtuous wealthy Romans. He was what extreme wealth produced in his era, the same way, it turns out, it produced similar outcomes in every era that followed.

Here is a short quiz. Read the following description and identify the historical period.

A small group of individuals has accumulated wealth so extreme that it is functionally incomprehensible to ordinary people. They have used that wealth to purchase political influence, suppress labor organizing, avoid taxation through legislative capture, and build physical monuments to their own magnificence. They throw parties so lavish that the food budget alone exceeds the annual income of everyone who prepared and served it. They have constructed an elaborate cultural mythology explaining why their success is a natural outcome of their superior virtues rather than a product of systematic advantage. They view reformers who want to redistribute some fraction of this concentration as dangerous radicals. Several of them have recently lost touch with basic social reality in ways their employees notice but are financially incentivized not to mention.

If you answered any decade from the last ten years, you are correct. If you answered the Gilded Age of the 1880s, you are also correct. If you answered the late Roman Republic, Bourbon France, Mughal India, feudal Europe, or pretty much any historical moment where wealth has concentrated significantly, you are still correct.

This is the most uncomfortable finding of the entire book, and we should name it clearly before proceeding: the behaviors documented in the previous three chapters are not modern. They are not the product of late-stage capitalism, social media, or the particular cultural conditions of the twenty-first century. They are what concentrated wealth and power have reliably produced in human beings across every civilization, every economic system, and every century for which we have records.

Which means they are not a bug. They are a feature. And they have been documented long enough that we should probably stop being surprised.

If you answered 'the last decade,' congratulations, you are correct.

If you answered 'the Gilded Age of the 1880s and 1890s,' you are also correct.

If you answered 'the late Roman Republic, roughly 133 to 27 BCE,' you are still correct.

If you answered 'feudal Europe,' 'Bourbon France,' 'Mughal India,' 'the antebellum American South,' or 'pretty much any time wealthy people have concentrated significant power in human civilization,' you have identified the pattern this chapter is about.

We have spent three chapters establishing that wealth and power do specific, documented things to the human brain: they suppress empathy, corrupt judgment, invite psychopathic personality structures, and produce a clinically identifiable deterioration in the qualities most essential to decent leadership. The question this chapter asks is: if this is a product of brain chemistry and environmental psychology, why does the resulting behavior look so consistent across wildly different cultures, economic systems, political structures, and centuries? The answer, as you have probably guessed, is that brain chemistry and environmental psychology don't change just because the toga gets replaced by a three-piece suit.

The playbook is the same. It has always been the same. Let's do the historical tour.

Rome: The Original 'Mission Accomplished' Moment

The Roman Republic ran, more or less functionally, for about five hundred years. It had its problems: slavery, conquest, periodic political violence, an electoral system that gave the wealthy dramatically disproportionate voting weight, but it maintained something resembling institutional checks on individual power for a remarkably long time. Then the money arrived.

After Rome's conquest of Carthage in 146 BCE and subsequent annexation of Greece and Spain's silver mines, wealth flooded into the city at volumes that had no precedent in Roman history. Plunder, tribute, slave labor, and provincial taxation generated fortunes for the senatorial elite that made even their previous wealthy selves look quaint. A small number of families, the optimates (Rome's conservative aristocratic faction), consolidated land, capital, and political machinery at a pace that the Republic's institutions simply had not been designed to manage.

What happened next is documented with impressive clarity in the historical record, because the Romans were excellent record-keepers and deeply interested in their own dysfunction. The senate became, in the words of one contemporary analyst quoted in Edward Watts's Mortal Republic, afflicted by 'unlimited and unrestrained greed that invaded, violated, and devastated everything, respecting nothing and holding nothing sacred.' Normal rules of political conduct (what the Romans called the mos maiorum, the unwritten codes of behavior that held the system together) began to erode, first at the edges, then systemically.

When the reformer Tiberius Gracchus proposed land redistribution to address the catastrophic inequality that was impoverishing Roman citizens and concentrating property in senatorial hands, the Senate had him killed. His brother Gaius Gracchus, who attempted similar reforms, was also killed. Their murderers were wealthy senators protecting their asset base. The response to reform proposals was not debate; it was assassination.

Over the following century, the concentration of wealth that had made individual senators richer than small nations also made them ungovernable by any institution theoretically superior to them. They hired private armies. They bribed courts.

They purchased elections. The general Sulla marched his legions on Rome itself in 87 BCE, the first time Roman soldiers turned their weapons on fellow Romans, to prevent a political rival from exercising legally granted authority. He then had himself declared dictator, compiled proscription lists of enemies to be murdered, and seized their property. Historians estimate he had approximately 1,500 senators and wealthy equestrians killed in this fashion. He used the proceeds to fund his political position.

Julius Caesar, observing this system from within, did not try to reform it. He out-maneuvered it, crossed the Rubicon with his army in 49 BCE in direct violation of Roman law, and within five years had himself declared dictator for life. He was assassinated in 44 BCE by senators who feared he was about to abolish the institution that gave them power, which, to be fair to the assassins, he probably was. What followed was twenty years of civil war and the permanent end of the Republic.

The core of this story is not military or political. It is psychological. The Roman elite, made extraordinarily wealthy by conquest, stopped perceiving institutional constraints as legitimate. They transgressed norms with increasing frequency and decreasing consequence. The unwritten rules that had maintained collective restraint dissolved because the incentive to maintain them vanished when individual wealth made defection from the collective more profitable than cooperation within it. The behavior was not unique to any individual senator or general. It was the predictable output of a system where concentrated wealth had eliminated the feedback mechanisms that previously kept behavior in check.

“The ancient sources called Rome’s dysfunction ‘moral decay from wealth and the hubris of Rome’s domination.’ Modern historians propose a more specific cause: the loss of elite cohesion from 133 BC, driven by wealth inequality and a growing willingness to transgress political norms.” (Wikipedia, citing scholarly consensus on the Crisis of the Roman Republic

The Roman Republic did not die because of external enemies. It died because its wealthiest members decided that the rules no longer applied to them. This conclusion, reached through the neurological processes described in chapters one through three, had predictable political consequences. It always does.

The Gilded Age: When History Didn’t Bother Disguising the Repeat

The American Gilded Age (roughly 1870 to 1900) is the most naked rerun of the Roman pattern in modern Western history, and the people living through it noticed. Mark Twain coined the term in 1873, titling a satirical novel The Gilded Age: A Tale of Today to describe an era where glittering surfaces concealed systemic rot. The University of Chicago later called Thorstein Veblen’s 1899 analysis of this world ‘a savage and frequently ironic assault on current values.’ These are not gentle descriptions from people who thought they were witnessing normal social development.

By 1890, the wealthiest one percent of American families controlled 51 percent of the nation's real and personal property. A small number of industrialists (Rockefeller, Carnegie, Vanderbilt, Morgan, Frick, Gould) had built monopolistic enterprises of a scale and political reach that functionally exceeded the capacity of federal institutions to regulate them. They did this, to quote the period's own critics, through 'speculating in dubious securities, bribing entire legislatures, and squeezing maximum productivity from their workers.'

The political capture was systematic and largely open. Railroad companies literally wrote the legislation governing their own operations. Senators were purchased with documented transparency; the phrase 'robber baron' was used not as a metaphor but as a description, comparing these industrialists to the feudal warlords who historically extracted tolls from travelers on bridges and roads they controlled. One historian of the period described the era's wealthy as 'playacting at aristocracy,' buying European titles, replicating Versailles in Newport mansions, importing medieval tapestries from noble families needing cash, and constructing a cultural performance of inherited legitimacy that the actual European aristocracy found laughably new-money.

Veblen watched this performance and wrote a book about it. The Theory of the Leisure Class (1899) gave the English language two concepts it has never since been able to do without: 'conspicuous consumption' and 'conspicuous leisure.' His argument was not that wealthy people were spending money on things (that's what money does). His argument was that the specific function of elite consumption had become primarily demonstrative rather than practical. The point of the yacht was not to sail it. The point was that other people could see you had it. Wealth had become primarily a signaling mechanism, a way of broadcasting social dominance that served the same function that physical dominance had served in earlier, more overtly predatory social arrangements.

Veblen was bracingly unsentimental about this. He traced the 'leisure class' back to what he called the 'predatory culture,' early social structures in which the primary social distinction was between those who hunted and fought (men) and those who did the productive work of sustaining life (everybody else). The leisure class, in Veblen's analysis, was a modernized version of the warrior class: exempt from productive labor, defined by conspicuous non-production, and legitimized by a cultural mythology that reframed predatory wealth accumulation as evidence of virtue rather than extraction. 'In order to gain and to hold the esteem of men,' Veblen wrote, 'it is not sufficient merely to possess wealth or power. The wealth or power must be put in evidence, for esteem is awarded only on evidence.'

The Gilded Age plutocrats were not, by and large, happy people doing interesting things with their money. They were anxious status competitors frantically signaling to each other through increasingly elaborate performances of conspicuous waste. Herman Melville, watching from the sidelines, called them 'such a mob of gilded dunces that not to be wealthy carries with it a certain distinction and nobility.' This was not a man impressed.

The progressive reforms that eventually constrained Gilded Age excess: antitrust legislation, the income tax, labor law reform, and food and drug safety, arrived not because the wealthy class discovered conscience. They arrived because the social pressure of organized labor movements, muckraking journalism, and political insurgency reached a threshold at which the cost of continued extraction exceeded the cost of conceding some fraction of it. The behavior changed when the structural incentives changed. The underlying psychology did not.

The Pattern Is the Point

Historians of different eras resist grand unified theories, for good professional reasons. The specific circumstances of late Republican Rome are not the same as Gilded Age America, which are not the same as feudal Europe, which are not the same as contemporary techno-plutocracy. Context matters. The differences are real and important.

But when you are looking for patterns of behavior (not policy specifics, not economic mechanics, but the human psychological responses to concentrated wealth and power), the similarities are more striking than the differences. Across all these contexts, several behavioral patterns appear with enough consistency to constitute something close to a law of elite behavior:

First: Wealthy elites consistently use their resources to capture the regulatory and legislative mechanisms designed to constrain them. This is not cynical conspiracy; it is rational incentive structure. If you can afford to purchase the process that sets your rules, purchasing that process is financially rational. The Roman senatorial class bought elections and courts. The robber barons bought legislators and wrote their own regulatory language. This is not a human failing unique to villains. It is what happens when one party to a political system has resources vastly exceeding those of any other party.

Second: As wealth concentrates and institutional constraint weakens, the behavior of the wealthy becomes progressively less tethered to the social reality of ordinary people. Roman senators in the final Republic were making decisions that caused mass civilian suffering without apparent awareness that the suffering was happening. Gilded Age industrialists deployed Pinkerton agents to shoot striking workers and seem to have experienced this as a management problem rather than a moral one. The contemporary equivalent, executives who have not personally encountered the consequences of their decisions for the people those decisions affect, is so ordinary it has stopped registering as remarkable.

Third: Every concentration of wealth at historically extreme levels has eventually generated a corrective response: reform movements, revolution, institutional restructuring, or some combination of the above. This has not always been pretty. Roman 'reform' produced a century of civil war. French reform produced the Terror. The corrective forces tend to be proportional to the accumulated grievance, which tends to be proportional to the original concentration and the duration of extraction.

Veblen's phrase 'conspicuous consumption' referred to spending that satisfies no need other than to build prestige. He traced this behavior to the same psychological structure as predatory social dominance, updated for an era of industrial capital.

Fourth, and perhaps most relevant to the argument of this book: each era produces a cultural mythology that explains the concentration of wealth as natural, earned, and beneficial. Roman senators were the natural leaders of civilization, their wealth proof of their military and civic virtue. Gilded Age industrialists were 'Captains of Industry,' building America's economic greatness, a framing so successfully marketed that it created the counter-debate about 'robber barons vs. captains of industry' that historians still cite. The contemporary mythology of the tech billionaire as visionary genius whose wealth is simply the market's recognition of his transformative value is a direct descendant of these earlier framings. The specific content changes. The function (providing ideological justification for extraction) does not.

Why This Keeps Happening and What It Tells Us

The historical pattern matters for one specific reason that makes it different from an interesting observation about human nature: it tells us this is not random. It is not a series of unfortunate coincidences produced by particularly bad individual actors. It is a structural output of conditions that recur.

The conditions are: a sufficiently extreme concentration of wealth relative to everyone else, sufficient duration of that concentration to allow institutional capture to take hold, and the removal of sufficient external constraints to allow the psychological changes documented in chapters one through three to compound without correction.

When these conditions exist (in Rome, in Gilded Age America, in contemporary concentrated techno-capital) the behavior follows. Not because all wealthy people are monsters (they aren't), not because extreme wealth inevitably produces pure evil (it doesn't), but because the neurological and institutional dynamics don't change based on whether the person experiencing them is wearing a toga or a $5,000 hoodie. The dopamine reward systems, the mirror neuron suppression, the hubris syndrome progression, the psychopathic trait amplification: all of these operate on the same biological hardware they have always operated on. The external circumstances are different. The internal machinery is not.

Edward Watts, the UC San Diego historian whose Mortal Republic chronicles the fall of the Roman Republic, drew the parallel explicitly when asked about contemporary relevance: 'What took place in Rome is a lesson for all modern republics.' His argument is not that history repeats mechanically. It is that the human psychological patterns that drive historical failure are consistent enough that documented historical outcomes can be read as early warning indicators.

The warning indicators are: extreme wealth concentration combined with political capture, combined with the normalization of elite impunity, combined with a cultural mythology that frames extraction as virtue. Rome had all four. The Gilded Age had all four. The question of whether any contemporary arrangement has all four is left, for the moment, as an exercise for the reader.

What the history tells us, unambiguously, is that this combination has never produced a stable, just, or sustainable social arrangement. It has always, eventually, produced a corrective response of some kind. The corrective responses have varied in character (reform, revolution, institutional collapse, or slow democratic restructuring), but the direction has been consistent: toward redistribution, accountability, and constraint.

Thorstein Veblen, watching the Gilded Age from a University of Chicago assistant professorship in 1899, wrote with what was described as 'one eye fixed on the squirming reader.' He was not optimistic about the leisure class's capacity for self-correction. He was, however, confident that the analysis itself was useful, that naming the pattern accurately was a prerequisite to doing anything about it.

We are still in the naming phase of this book. The patterns are: documented, repeated, consistent, and grounded in mechanisms that we now understand neurologically rather than merely observationally. Veblen had the observational data.

We have the neuroscience. Together, they constitute a fairly comprehensive account of why the people at the top behave the way they do, and why they have always behaved more or less this way.

What to do about it is Chapter Eleven's problem. First, there are seven more things to explain.

Rome. The Gilded Age. The present. The same cycle, running on the same human neural hardware, producing the same outcomes across every economic system and century for which we have records. The Wealth Insanity Cycle is not a modern invention. It is an old machine that we have simply gotten better at documenting. Stages Four and Five, Empathy Erosion and Moral Disengagement, are where the documentation gets both more recent and more precise.

Chapter 5

The Myth Machine

How Society Learned to Love the People Robbing It

"If you can convince the lowest white man he's better than the best colored man, he won't notice you're picking his pocket. Hell, give him somebody to look down on and he'll empty his pockets for you." — Lyndon B. Johnson, 1960. He was not being complimentary.

Here is a question that should bother you more than it probably does.

The previous four chapters have established, with peer-reviewed receipts, that extreme wealth and institutional power reliably produce a specific constellation of psychological outcomes: dopamine dysregulation, empathy erosion, psychopathic trait amplification, hubris syndrome, moral disengagement, and a historical track record of these patterns stretching back to the first civilizations that figured out how to accumulate capital. The research is robust. The pattern is consistent. The mechanisms are documented.

So why does everyone keep letting it happen?

Not just 'letting it happen' in the passive sense of failing to stop it. Actively facilitating it. Voting for it. Defending it. Celebrating it. Building parasocial relationships with billionaires on social media and feeling genuine outrage when anyone suggests that a person who could buy a small country should maybe pay more in taxes. Working seventy hours a week for a company that will lay you off by spreadsheet while simultaneously believing that the people at the top got there through superior merit and that you could be one of them if you just worked a little harder.

That last part is the interesting one. Because it is not an accident.

The Wealth Insanity Cycle, described in the Introduction, runs through six stages. Stages One through Five (dopamine capture, power poisoning, psychopathic selection, empathy erosion, moral disengagement) explain what happens inside the people accumulating wealth and power. Stage Six, System Capture, is where those individuals reshape the institutions around them to protect and perpetuate the conditions that produced them.

This chapter is about one specific and underexamined dimension of Stage Six: the manufacturing of the story that makes everyone else okay with it. The ideology. The narrative infrastructure. The myth.

Call it the Myth Machine. It has been running for a very long time, and it is considerably more sophisticated than a simple lie.

The Meritocracy Story: And Why It's Doing So Much Work

The word 'meritocracy' was coined in 1958 by a British sociologist named Michael Young, in a satirical novel called The Rise of the Meritocracy. Young imagined a dystopian future society in which status was allocated entirely by measured intelligence and effort, and depicted this as a catastrophe. The satirical point was that a system that genuinely allocated rewards by merit would be crueler than aristocracy, because aristocracy at least acknowledged that the system was rigged. Meritocracy told the losers it was their fault.

The word escaped its satirical context almost immediately and became the sincere description of what American capitalism was supposed to be. Young spent the rest of his life being furious about this. In a 2001 Guardian essay written three years before his death, he noted with dismay that the word he'd invented as a warning had been adopted as an aspiration. 'It is good sense,' he wrote, 'to appoint individual people to jobs on their merit. It is the opposite when those who are judged to have merit of a particular kind harden into a new social class without room in it for others.'

He was describing exactly what happened.

The empirical case against meritocracy as a description of how wealth is actually distributed in the United States is now substantial. Raj Chetty and his colleagues at Opportunity Insights have spent a decade building one of the most rigorous longitudinal datasets in economics, tracking the relationship between parental income and children's economic outcomes across millions of Americans. The findings are consistent and not subtle: the single strongest predictor of where you end up in the income distribution is where you started. Intergenerational income mobility, the likelihood of a child born to low-income parents reaching the top income quintile, is dramatically lower in the United States than in most comparable wealthy countries. The 'American Dream' of upward mobility through individual effort is, empirically, more achievable in Denmark.

This is not a new finding. It is a well-replicated finding that has been available to anyone paying attention for decades. Which raises the question: why does the meritocracy narrative persist so effectively in the face of evidence that it is, at best, a substantial exaggeration?

The myth of meritocracy isn't a mistake. It's load-bearing infrastructure. Remove it, and you have to explain why things are the way they are, and that explanation is considerably more uncomfortable.

The answer involves several interlocking psychological mechanisms, each of which has been studied in its own right and each of which is doing specific work in maintaining a story that serves the interests of the people at the top of the distribution far more than anyone else.

Just World Belief: The Psychological Engine

In 1965, a social psychologist named Melvin Lerner ran a study that produced results uncomfortable enough that he spent the next fifteen years trying to explain them.

Lerner showed participants a video of a woman receiving electric shocks as part of what appeared to be a learning experiment. The participants could not help her. Some were subsequently told she would be compensated for her suffering; others were not. The participants who were told she would not be compensated did something unexpected: they didn't express more sympathy for her. They derogated her. They rated her as less likeable, less admirable, and, notably, as somehow deserving of her fate.

Lerner called this the 'just world hypothesis': the cognitive tendency to believe that the world is fundamentally fair, that people get what they deserve and deserve what they get. It is, he argued, a psychological defense mechanism rather than an empirical observation. Believing in a just world allows people to feel safe: if bad things happen to people who deserve them, and I don't deserve bad things, I am protected. The alternative, that bad things happen randomly, or structurally, or as the result of systems that don't particularly care about individual desert, is genuinely terrifying in a way that the human brain goes to considerable lengths to avoid.

The just world belief produces a specific and well-documented cognitive distortion: the tendency to attribute outcomes to character rather than circumstance. The poor are poor because of choices they made. The rich are rich because of qualities they have. The suffering person in Lerner's video must have done something to end up there. The billionaire must have done something extraordinary to end up there.

This belief is not limited to conservatives, to the wealthy, or to people who haven't thought carefully about inequality. It is a baseline cognitive tendency that operates across political affiliations and income levels, requires active effort to counteract, and is strengthened by environments that emphasize individual agency and weaken structural explanations. The United States, which has historically placed unusually strong cultural emphasis on individual effort and unusually weak institutional emphasis on structural barriers, is a particularly effective incubator of just world belief.

Psychologist Claudia Dalbert and her colleagues have now published decades of research on just world belief and its correlates. The pattern is consistent: strong just world belief predicts reduced empathy for disadvantaged groups, increased victim blaming, stronger opposition to redistributive policies, and greater deference to authority and institutional hierarchies. It is, in short, psychologically useful for maintaining arrangements that benefit people at the top, not because those people conspired to produce just world belief, but because the belief system that makes people feel safe in an unequal world is also the belief system that makes them unlikely to challenge the inequality.

new section called 'The Language of Inevitability' before 'The Lottery Ticket Problem'.

There is a specific linguistic feature of the Myth Machine that deserves its own attention before we move on: the systematic use of language that frames the current economic arrangement as natural, inevitable, and ungoverned by human agency.

Listen carefully to how extreme wealth is discussed in mainstream media and political discourse. Markets 'correct.' Wealth 'flows' to the most efficient uses. Jobs are 'created' by successful businesses. Companies 'need' to cut costs. The economy 'requires' certain conditions to grow.

These are not neutral descriptions. They are framings that attribute to economic arrangements the character of natural forces (things that happen independently of decisions, like weather or gravity) rather than the character of policy choices, which is what they actually are.

Linguist George Lakoff has spent decades documenting how conceptual metaphors (the deep structural analogies through which people understand abstract concepts) shape what policy responses seem natural and what seem absurd. When the economy is understood as a natural system, intervention feels unnatural. When wealth 'flows,' taxing it feels like damming a river. When markets 'correct,' regulation feels like interference with a self-healing organism. The metaphors do political work without making political arguments. They don't tell you what to think. They determine what seems thinkable.

The economists call this 'naturalization': the process by which contingent institutional arrangements, things built by people making choices under particular historical conditions that could be built differently, acquire the status of natural facts. French sociologist Pierre Bourdieu spent much of his career documenting how naturalization operates across class systems. His concept of 'doxa' (the realm of things that go without saying, that seem so obvious they require no defense, captures exactly the mechanism. When an arrangement achieves doxa status, challenging it doesn't feel like a political disagreement. It feels like denying gravity.

The current American economic arrangement, in which the top one percent holds more wealth than the bottom fifty percent combined, in which real wages for the median worker have been largely flat for forty years while corporate profits have tripled, in which a person's zip code at birth is the single strongest predictor of their lifetime earnings, has achieved something close to doxa status in mainstream political discourse. It is not debated as a policy outcome that could be different. It is described as the background condition against which policy operates. The specific people and decisions that produced it have been dissolved into the passive voice and the language of necessity.

The most effective political move is not to win an argument. It is to define the terrain on which arguments are allowed to happen. The Myth Machine doesn't need to convince anyone of anything specific. It needs to maintain the sense that the current arrangement is what normal looks like.

This is also why the strongest challenges to extreme wealth concentration tend to generate such visceral resistance, not just from the wealthy but from people who would materially benefit from the changes being proposed. Challenging the arrangement feels like challenging reality. The psychological discomfort of just world disruption, the cognitive cost of revising a doxa, and the social risk of breaking from apparent consensus all activate simultaneously. It's not that the opposition is stupid or confused. It's that the Myth Machine has been running on their cognitive hardware long enough to feel like their own thinking.

arrangement feel illegitimate before anyone has looked at the paragraph:

None of this is permanent. Doxa fractures when reality becomes undeniable, when the gap between the story and lived experience becomes too wide to paper over with rhetoric. The 2008 financial crisis cracked it briefly; the decade following produced a measurable shift in public attitudes toward wealth concentration. The COVID-19 pandemic cracked it again: essential workers were redefined as essential, visibly, while people with laptops and investment portfolios found the arrangement remarkably survivable. Each crack is an opportunity. The Myth Machine is durable but not invincible. Its vulnerability is the same as its mechanism: it runs on belief, and beliefs can change when the evidence against them becomes personal.

The Lottery Ticket Problem

There is a second mechanism at work, distinct from just world belief but reinforcing it: the enduring appeal of the possibility of joining the wealthy class, even when the probability of doing so is vanishingly small.

Behavioral economists have documented this extensively. People systematically overestimate their own probability of achieving extreme success. They buy lottery tickets. They believe their startup will be the one that makes it. They watch billionaire interviews and absorb the origin story (the dorm room, the garage, the early failure and subsequent persistence) and locate themselves in that narrative rather than in the statistical distribution that says most dorm rooms and garages produce neither billion-dollar companies nor meaningful financial security.

This is not stupidity. It is a predictable outcome of several well-documented cognitive biases operating together. Availability bias: the billionaire's origin story is extremely available, appearing on magazine covers, in commencement speeches, and in the cultural narrative, while the millions of equally hardworking people who didn't make it are not. Optimism bias: people reliably believe their outcomes will be better than the base rate predicts. And specifically relevant here, what psychologists call 'system justification': the tendency to support existing social arrangements as legitimate and desirable, partly because believing the system is fair reduces the psychological distress of living inside it.

The lottery ticket problem has a specific political consequence. When people believe they might one day be wealthy, they tend to adopt the political preferences of people who are currently wealthy, including preferences for lower taxes on high incomes and wealth, weaker labor protections, and reduced social safety nets. You don't vote to tax the rich if you think you might be rich someday. This has been documented empirically. Economists Andrew Achen and Larry Bartels, in their 2016 book Democracy for Realists, established that voters systematically vote against their material economic interests when their identity affiliations and aspirational self-concepts point in a different direction.

The most effective thing the wealthy class ever did for its own preservation was convince everyone else that they were temporarily embarrassed members of it.

The phrase 'temporarily embarrassed millionaires' has been attributed, probably apocryptally, to John Steinbeck, but the underlying observation predates any specific attribution and has been confirmed empirically. It is not that working people are foolish. It is that the psychological machinery of aspiration, identity, and just world belief combines to make solidarity with the people above you feel more natural than solidarity with the people next to you.

The Media Architecture of Deference

Manufactured consent (the phrase comes from Noam Chomsky and Edward Herman's 1988 book of the same name, drawing on Walter Lippmann's earlier concept of 'the manufacture of consent') is sometimes read as a conspiracy theory: a coordinated effort by media owners to suppress information unfavorable to their class interests. The actual argument is more subtle and considerably more disturbing than that.

Chomsky and Herman proposed a 'propaganda model,' not in the sense of deliberate disinformation, but in the sense of structural filters that shape what information gets produced, amplified, and consumed without requiring anyone to explicitly coordinate the suppression of anything. The five filters they identified in 1988 are worth reviewing, because they have only become more accurate with time: ownership concentration (the outlets that reach the most people are owned by the people with the most capital); advertising dependence (revenue comes from selling audiences to advertisers, who are also businesses with interests); sourcing (the most efficient sources of news are institutional (corporations, government agencies, think tanks), all of which have resources and interests that shape what they make available); flak (the organized pushback against coverage unfavorable to powerful interests, which shapes editorial decisions prospectively); and ideology (the set of background assumptions about what is normal, natural, and inevitable that define the terms of acceptable debate).

The propaganda model doesn't require editors to receive phone calls from billionaire owners telling them what to run. It predicts that the structural incentives of a commercially funded media system will produce coverage that is systematically more favorable to the interests of wealthy institutions than its stated objectivity norms would suggest, and that this will happen without most of the journalists involved being aware of it, because the filters operate at the level of what questions get asked, what sources get consulted, and what frameworks get applied rather than at the level of explicit instruction.

The empirical research on media coverage and economic interests is consistent with this model. Studies of coverage of labor disputes, tax policy debates, and economic inequality consistently find that coverage emphasizes business perspectives, uses business-sourced data, and frames economic issues through the lens of business impact rather than worker or community impact, not because of any coordinated effort, but because the structural incentives of commercially-funded journalism point systematically in that direction.

This matters for the Myth Machine because the media is where most people encounter the narratives about wealth, success, and economic arrangement that shape their beliefs about what is normal and what is possible. A media ecosystem that structurally overrepresents wealthy perspectives will produce a population with a distorted picture of how wealth is created, distributed, and sustained, not through lies exactly, but through emphasis, framing, and the systematic underdevelopment of alternatives.

What the Myth Does to the Rest of Us

The cumulative effect of just world belief, the lottery ticket problem, and media-architecture deference is a population that is considerably harder to organize around material interests than its actual economic situation would suggest it should be.

This is not a new observation. Labor historians have been making it for over a century. What has changed is the quality of the psychological and neuroscientific evidence explaining the mechanisms. We now understand considerably better than previous generations did why the appeal to class interest has always been less politically effective than the appeal to identity, aspiration, and group membership that cuts across class lines.

Political scientist Larry Bartels, in his 2008 book Unequal Democracy, documented one of the most striking empirical patterns in modern political science: the consistent failure of economic self-interest to predict voting behavior in the way that economic theory would predict. Working-class voters who would materially benefit from redistributive policies reliably do not vote for them at the rates their interests would suggest. The gap is not explained by ignorance; it is explained by identity, by aspiration, and by the just world mechanisms that make deference to hierarchy feel more natural than challenge to it.

The Myth Machine doesn't need to convince anyone of anything false. It just needs to maintain a set of background assumptions (that the system is basically fair, that success reflects merit, that extreme wealth is the result of extraordinary contribution, that structural critique is the province of people who couldn't compete) that make challenging the arrangement feel illegitimate before anyone has looked at the evidence.

Chapter Five examines the mechanism that makes this particularly effective: the systematic erosion of the empathy that would otherwise make the human cost of these arrangements emotionally legible. The Myth Machine provides the ideology. The empathy erosion provides the insulation. Together, they are very efficient.

Chapter 6

The Empathy Gap

How Power Rewires the Brain's Social Software

It's not that they don't care. It's that they've become neurologically incapable of noticing there's something to care about.

Picture a busy four-way intersection in the San Francisco Bay Area. Cars take turns, mostly. A pedestrian steps off the curb and waits for a gap in traffic to cross.

Now picture what happens next, sorted by the car the driver is sitting in.

Drivers of older, cheaper vehicles? They yield. They stop. They wave the pedestrian across. This is common. This is normal.

Drivers of newer, more expensive vehicles (the BMWs, the Mercedes, the Audis) are statistically, measurably, significantly more likely to drive straight through the crosswalk. Some make eye contact with the waiting pedestrian first. Then they drive through anyway.

This is not an anecdote. This is a published result from a peer-reviewed study in the Proceedings of the National Academy of Sciences, one of the most prestigious scientific journals in the world. Researchers Paul Piff, Daniel Stancato, Stéphane Côté, Rodolfo Mendoza-Denton, and Dacher Keltner sat at intersections and recorded 274 drivers, rating vehicle status on a five-point scale and watching who followed the law. Drivers of the highest-status vehicles were four times more likely to cut off other cars and significantly more likely to bypass waiting pedestrians, even after making eye contact. The eye contact part matters. It means they saw the person. They just didn't respond to seeing them the way the rest of us respond to seeing a person.

That gap, between perceiving another person's existence and caring about it, is what this chapter is about. And it turns out it is not a character flaw. It is not cruelty in the traditional sense. It is, in a very specific and now well-documented way, a measurable product of what wealth does to the brain's empathy systems over time.

If the previous chapters described how wealth corrupts judgment, inflates ego, and builds psychopathic organizational cultures, this chapter describes the mechanism underneath all of it: the gradual erosion of the cognitive and emotional infrastructure through which one human being recognizes and cares about the experience of another. Empathy is not just a feeling. It is a skill. And like any skill, it requires practice, need, and the right environmental conditions to develop and maintain. Wealth, it turns out, systematically removes all three.

The Research That Should Embarrass Everyone Who Ever Praised the Wealthy for Their Generosity

Dacher Keltner is a professor of psychology at UC Berkeley and one of the most productive researchers in the field of emotion and social behavior. He has spent the better part of two decades studying the relationship between social class and empathy. His lab's findings, replicated across more than a dozen separate studies, add up to something that should be uncomfortable for any society that asks its wealthiest members to voluntarily give back: wealthy people are measurably less good at feeling, recognizing, and responding to the emotional states of others.

The foundational study on facial expression recognition came from Keltner's lab in 2010, when Michael Kraus, Stéphane Côté, and Keltner published 'Social Class, Contextualism, and Empathic Accuracy' in Psychological Science. Across three studies, they established a consistent pattern: lower-class individuals outperformed upper-class individuals on every measure of empathic accuracy they tested.

In the first study, participants completed a standardized test measuring how accurately they could infer another person's emotional state. Lower-class participants scored significantly higher. In the second study, pairs of strangers were brought in and had conversations. Lower-class participants were more accurate at inferring what their conversation partner was actually feeling during the interaction. In the third study, notably, participants were shown photographs of eyes only. Just the eyes, nothing else. They were asked to identify the emotion being expressed. Lower-class participants were more accurate. Photographs of eyes. Not even full faces. The difference in empathic attunement was visible at the level of reading subtle emotional cues from a strip of another person's face.

The explanation Kraus and Keltner offered is structural, not moral. Lower-class individuals, they argued, live in environments where other people matter a great deal to their outcomes. When you cannot easily control your environment through resources, you have to manage it through social intelligence. You need to know when your boss is in a bad mood before you ask for something. You need to know when a colleague is sympathetic versus hostile. You need to read the room, constantly, because the room has consequences that money cannot insulate you from. Upper-class individuals, by contrast, have the resources to override or ignore social friction. If a relationship gets awkward, you can hire someone else. If a neighbor is hostile, you can move. The need to accurately perceive other people's emotional states is structurally lower when you're wealthy. So the skill atrophies.

'Lower class people just show more empathy,' Keltner said flatly in an interview. 'No matter how you look at it.'

This is the Berkeley lab director. This is not a political activist. This is a researcher who has spent his career measuring this, and who keeps getting the same answer.

"Our data say you cannot rely on the wealthy to give back." — Dacher Keltner, UC Berkeley, summarizing over a decade of research on social class and compassion

Your Heart Rate Is an Honest Witness

Subjective self-report is an imperfect research tool. People lie. People rationalize. People genuinely don't know what they feel. This is especially true for wealthy people assessing their own empathy, because, as we'll get to, wealthy people tend to overestimate their own sensitivity while underestimating their actual behavioral response to others' suffering.

This is why the physiological studies matter so much.

Jennifer Stellar, a social psychologist who did her doctoral work at UC Berkeley with Keltner and Kraus, ran a study that used heart rate monitors to cut through the problem of self-report. Published in 2012 in the journal Emotion under the title 'Class and Compassion: Socioeconomic Factors Predict Responses to Suffering,' the study brought participants into a lab and showed them two videos. One video was neutral: a man explaining how to build a patio. The other was emotionally charged: families coping with having a child with cancer. Heart rates were monitored throughout.

The participants all said, afterward, that the cancer video had made them sad. All of them. Across social classes, people reported being moved by children suffering from cancer. Of course they did. That's what you're supposed to say, and that's also probably what they believed. But the heart monitors told a more precise story.

When lower-class participants watched the cancer video, their heart rates slowed. This is the physiological signature of compassion, a parasympathetic response associated with paying close, engaged attention to another person's suffering, opening yourself to it rather than shutting it out. The technical term is heart rate deceleration. In everyday language, it means: their bodies were actually responding to the suffering on screen.

Upper-class participants' heart rates, when watching the same video, generally did not change.

Let that sit for a moment. Lower-class participants weren't just reporting more compassion. Their autonomic nervous systems were producing the physiological response associated with compassion. Upper-class participants were producing the verbal report ('yes, of course the cancer video moved me') without the accompanying bodily response.

Stellar was careful, in subsequent interviews, to be precise about what this means and what it doesn't. 'It's not, I can see you're suffering. I can tell. But I don't care,' she explained. 'They're just not attuned to it.' This is a crucial distinction. The finding is not that wealthy people are secretly indifferent and pretending otherwise. It is that the attunement process, the mechanism by which you pick up on another person's suffering and allow it to register in your own body, is operating at lower intensity. The signal isn't being suppressed. It's not getting through in the first place.

The same study also found that, in one of three experiments, the class difference in empathic behavior was eliminated when participants were first asked to write about the feelings of a suffering person before making decisions that affected them. The moment upper-class participants were prompted to deliberately attend to someone else's emotional experience, the class gap in compassionate behavior largely vanished. The capacity was there. The default orientation was not.

What this means, practically, is that the empathy problem of the wealthy is not a fixed trait but a calibration problem. Their attunement defaults are set lower. They don't spontaneously tune in to others' emotional frequencies the way people who've spent their lives needing to. This should be less reassuring than it sounds, because most of the decisions that affect millions of people are made by wealthy individuals operating in their default mode, not in carefully prompted experimental conditions.

Seven Studies and a Crosswalk

The Piff et al. PNAS study that opened this chapter was not a single study. It was seven, which is unusual, and it was designed to be unusual for a reason: the researchers wanted to make it as hard as possible to dismiss the finding as a fluke or a methodological artifact. Seven studies, using both naturalistic field observation and controlled laboratory experiments, testing unethical behavior across multiple domains, with samples from both university populations and a nationwide database.

Studies 1 and 2 were the intersection observations: the crosswalk and the four-way stop, watching real drivers in real traffic to assess law-breaking behavior. Studies 3 through 7 moved into the laboratory. Study 3 gave participants vignettes describing workplace scenarios and asked them to rate the likelihood they would engage in various ethically questionable behaviors; upper-class participants indicated higher likelihood. Study 4 gave participants a candy jar labeled as belonging to children and left them alone with it; they were told anything remaining would go to kids in a nearby study. Upper-class participants took more candy. Study 5 asked participants to play a negotiation game and found that upper-class individuals were more likely to lie about their goals. Study 6 was a dice game where participants reported their own rolls (higher scores won cash prizes); the distribution of reported scores among upper-class participants was statistically impossible given a fair die, indicating cheating. Study 7 surveyed employees directly about their workplace behavior; upper-class respondents endorsed unethical conduct at work at higher rates.

Across all seven studies, the pattern held: the higher the social class, the greater the inclination toward behavior that benefited the self at the cost of others.

The mediating factor, the thing the data pointed to as the mechanism, was attitudes toward greed. Upper-class participants held more favorable views of greed as a legitimate motivator. And those favorable views toward greed predicted the unethical behavior. As Piff described it, 'The relative privilege and security enjoyed by upper-class individuals give rise to independence from others and a prioritization of the self and one's own welfare over the welfare of others, what we call greed.'

Plato, Piff noted with some relish, had identified greed as the root of personal immorality around 380 BCE. It took psychology until 2012 to run the controlled experiments, but the conclusion held up.

There were subsequent replication challenges, as there are with virtually all social psychology findings of this scope. A 2017 preregistered replication found no relationship between vehicle status and cutting off pedestrians in one sample; other research replicated the pedestrian-yielding findings. The academic consensus, as of this writing, is that the pattern is real but the effect size varies by context and the specific nature of the class manipulation matters. For our purposes, what matters is that the overall body of evidence (the empathic accuracy studies, the physiological compassion studies, the behavioral ethics studies) converges on the same conclusion from multiple methodological directions. This convergence is not easy to dismiss.

The Self-Report Trap and Why Wealthy People Think They're More Empathetic Than They Are

There is a particularly cruel irony embedded in this research that deserves its own section.

Neural research on social class and empathy, specifically ERP (event-related potential) studies measuring brain activity in response to images of suffering, has found that higher socioeconomic status is associated with diminished neural empathic responses, as measured by a marker called fronto-central P2. This is the electrical brain signature of attending to and processing another person's pain. Wealthy participants show smaller P2 responses to images of painful faces.

But here is the part that will make you set the book down for a moment: the same research found that higher socioeconomic status was positively correlated with self-reported trait empathy.

Read that again. Wealthy people score lower on objective neurological measures of empathic response. And they score higher on surveys asking how empathetic they think they are.

They do not know. They genuinely believe they are highly empathetic, sensitive, and responsive to others' needs. Their brains are producing less empathic neural activity when shown people in pain, and simultaneously they are filling out personality surveys saying they are very caring individuals. This is not strategic dishonesty. This is a gap between self-perception and neurological reality that wealth has created, and that the social environments of wealth consistently reinforce. No one around them is telling them otherwise, partly because people below them in the hierarchy have significant financial disincentives to deliver that feedback, and partly because the performance of empathy in wealthy social contexts (the charity gala, the corporate social responsibility statement, the philanthropic foundation bearing one's name) is so elaborate and visible that it is easily mistaken, even by the person doing it, for the actual thing.

Keltner's observation about this is blunt: 'The rich tend to gloss over the way family connections, money and education contribute to their lives, resulting in less empathy.' The glossing over is not false modesty in reverse. It is a genuine cognitive pattern, a tendency to explain one's own outcomes in terms of personal virtue and talent rather than structural advantage. And that attribution pattern, consistently applied over years or decades, produces a self-image of a self-made person whose success is evidence of their quality. From there, it is a short psychological step to the conclusion that people who have not succeeded have not done so because of their lower quality, which is not a foundation from which genuine compassion is easily extended.

Michael Kraus framed the empathy capacity this way: 'What our research is suggesting is that upper class people don't have a lower capacity for empathy. They just pay less attention. And if you can put them in a situation where you get them to pay more attention, you can get some real empathy from people who are wealthy and affluent.' This is important. The empathy hardware is not broken. The default settings are badly calibrated. The question of whether that distinction is meaningful in practice is, again, a question about who is doing the recalibrating, whether the structural conditions that created the miscalibration are ever addressed, and what happens to the millions of people affected by decisions made in the miscalibrated default state.

Higher socioeconomic status is associated with diminished neural empathic responses, and simultaneously with higher self-reported empathy. The people whose brains are reacting least to others' pain believe themselves to be among the most caring.

What This Means When the Decisions Are Real

The crosswalk study is vivid and digestible, which is why it tends to dominate the popular coverage of this research. But the crosswalk is not where the stakes are.

The stakes are in the boardroom where wage structures are decided. They are in the legislature where tax policy is written by representatives funded by people whose empathic neural responses are running at reduced output. They are in the venture capital meeting where a founder pitches a product that will affect the daily lives of tens of millions of people, and the decision about whether to fund it is made by someone whose heart rate did not slow down during the cancer video.

Keltner said this explicitly, in terms that are not subtle: 'People in positions of power are not going to see the inequality. They're going to be blind to it and that has enormous implications for how we educate leaders, why they may not see what's obvious to everyone else and why they may not even understand the suffering of the people below them.'

The word 'blind' here is almost literal. The research is not describing people who see suffering and choose not to care. It is describing a condition in which the signal of suffering does not reliably reach the level of conscious attention in the first place. The crosswalk pedestrian is visible (upper-class drivers make eye contact, remember), but the significance of that person's experience does not register with the same urgency it registers for lower-class drivers. Scale that attunement gap up to the level of policy decisions affecting populations, and you have a structural problem with a neurological root.

The structural implication that Keltner and Kraus draw from their research: that 'you cannot rely on the wealthy to give back' is not cynicism. It is an evidence-based conclusion about default behavior in the absence of structural incentives or deliberate intervention. The wealthy can and do behave generously, particularly when prompted, when social visibility makes generosity a performance that earns status, or when they have found unusual ways to maintain empathic attunement despite the structural conditions that erode it. But the default, absent these correcting factors, trends toward self-focus.

The Piff lab's Monopoly experiment captures this neatly, even if it's an oversimplification. Participants were randomly assigned to be either the wealthy or the poor player in a rigged game where the wealthy player had double the starting money, collected twice the salary, and rolled with two dice against the poor player's one. The wealthy players, over time, began to behave as though their position was deserved. They moved their pieces more aggressively. They took more food from a shared bowl. They attributed their eventual victory, statistically guaranteed by the rules, to their own skill and strategic decision-making. When the experiment ended and the structural rigging was explained, many wealthy players genuinely seemed surprised. They had, within the span of a twenty-minute board game, begun to feel as though they had earned what was simply given to them.

This is, in miniature, the story of empathy and wealth. Resources produce independence. Independence produces self-focus. Self-focus produces attunement atrophy. Attunement atrophy produces reduced sensitivity to others' suffering. And across the whole arc, the person experiencing this shift has no particular reason to notice it happening, because the shift feels like confidence, like success, like the natural state of someone who has earned their place.

It doesn't feel like losing something. It never does.

The Berkeley drivers who made eye contact with the pedestrian and then drove through anyway were not performing cruelty. They had simply lost, through a documented and measurable process, the automatic response that converts seeing another person into caring about them. Stage Four of the Cycle has been confirmed in labs, at intersections, and in brain imaging studies. Stage Five, Moral Disengagement, is what happens when the empathy deficit encounters a situation that would otherwise require an ethical response.

Chapter 7

The Rules Are for You

Entitlement, Moral Disengagement, and the Ethics of Other People

Laws are like Terms and Conditions. Nobody reads them, but only one group can actually ignore them.

Most people learn, at some early point in their lives, that rules apply to them. This lesson is usually delivered through consequences: a detention, a fine, a failed class, a relationship that ended badly, a moment where the abstraction of 'rules exist for a reason' became suddenly, personally concrete. The lesson sticks because consequences are good teachers. You touch the hot stove once.

The problem with being very wealthy is that you stop touching hot stoves. Not because you become more careful. Because someone else removes all the stoves from your vicinity, and replaces them with something that looks like a stove but does not burn. Over time, the cognitive architecture built around 'consequences exist and will occur to me' begins to atrophy from disuse. Not because wealthy people are uniquely malicious. Because the feedback loop that maintains that architecture in the rest of us has been systematically disconnected.

The result is a specific and well-documented cognitive profile: a genuine, functional belief that rules operate differently depending on who you are.

Not as a conscious philosophy. As an operating assumption so deeply embedded that it feels like simple observation of how the world works.

This is what it looked like, with particular clarity, on June 15, 2013, in Keller, Texas.

A sixteen-year-old named Ethan Couch stole two cases of beer from a Walmart, drank himself to a blood alcohol level of 0.24, three times the legal adult limit, loaded several teenagers into the bed of his family's pickup truck, and drove at 70 miles per hour through a 40-mph zone. He struck and killed four people: a pastor, his son's friend, and a woman and her daughter who had stopped to help with a disabled vehicle on the shoulder. Seven others were injured. One teenager in the truck bed was thrown clear and suffered a brain injury that left him permanently unable to speak or move.

Ethan Couch was sentenced to ten years of probation. No prison time. A stay at a private rehabilitation facility in Newport Beach, California, whose annual cost of $450,000 would be paid by his father's sheet metal business.

The defense argument that produced this sentence was not that Couch was innocent. It was that he was a victim of his own wealth. Defense psychologist G. Dick Miller testified that Couch suffered from 'affluenza': a condition in which extreme wealth and its accompanying absence of consequences had produced a young man who genuinely could not link his actions to their outcomes. The Couch household, Miller explained, had not taught the golden rule. It had taught a different one: 'We have the gold. We make the rules.'

The outrage was immediate. But the outrage missed something important. The affluenza defense was not an invention. It was an accurate description of a real phenomenon, documented in labs, measured in behavioral studies, and observable in institutions far more powerful than one Texas family's sheet metal business.

Ethan Couch was sentenced to ten years of probation.

No prison time. Ten years of probation, plus a stay at a private rehabilitation facility in Newport Beach, California, whose annual cost of $450,000 was to be paid by his father's successful sheet metal business. When news spread of his sentence, the outrage was, as The New York Times put it, 'emotional and angry and stretched far beyond the North Texas suburbs.' The victims' families watched the coverage and arrived at the only logical conclusion available to them. Eric Boyles, whose wife and daughter had both died in the crash, said it directly: 'Money always seems to keep this kid out of trouble. Ultimately today, I felt that money did prevail.'

What made the sentence internationally infamous was not merely its leniency. It was the argument that produced it. Defense psychologist G. Dick Miller had testified that Ethan Couch was a victim of 'affluenza,' a term he used to describe a condition in which extreme wealth and its accompanying lack of consequences had produced a young man who genuinely could not link his actions to their outcomes. Miller's description of the Couch household was precise: 'Instead of the golden rule, which was do unto others as you would have them do unto you, Couch was taught: we have the gold, we make the rules.' The parents, Miller explained, had taught their son 'a system that's 180 degrees from rational. If you hurt someone, say you're sorry. In that family, if you hurt someone, send some money.'

The 'affluenza' defense was widely ridiculed as a cynical legal gambit when it was introduced, and the mockery was largely deserved. The term itself is not a recognized clinical diagnosis. Miller later said publicly that he wished he had never used the word. The underlying phenomenon he was describing, however, the cognitive and behavioral consequence of growing up in an environment where consequences simply do not apply to you, is neither invented nor unique to Ethan Couch. It has a substantial scientific literature, a documented neurological mechanism, and a name that does not require air quotes: entitlement.

This chapter is about entitlement, about what it does to ethical reasoning, and about the psychological mechanism, Albert Bandura's moral disengagement, through which otherwise intelligent people commit serious harms and experience no internal conflict about having done so. Ethan Couch is the extreme version of a story that plays out across every level of concentrated wealth, from the teenager who can't link crashing a truck to consequences, to the CEO who can't link laying off thirty thousand workers to the suffering that follows. The mechanism is the same. The scale is just different.

Architecture

Adam Neumann co-founded WeWork in 2010. By 2019, the company was valued at $47 billion, making it one of the most valuable private companies in the world. It was also losing approximately $3,500 per minute. The IPO filing, when it was released in August 2019, was one of the stranger documents in the history of American corporate finance: a 350-page prospectus that used the word 'community' 150 times, described WeWork as 'a physical social network,' and revealed a corporate governance structure so tilted toward Neumann's personal control that it gave him shares with ten times the voting power of ordinary stockholders.

The filing also revealed, among other things, that Neumann had: trademarked the word 'We' and then sold the trademark back to his own company for $5.9 million; leased four buildings he personally owned to WeWork, collecting rent from a company he controlled; borrowed hundreds of millions of dollars from WeWork's lenders using his WeWork shares as collateral; and structured the company's governance so that if he died or became incapacitated, his wife Rebekah would have the right to select his replacement as CEO.

The IPO was withdrawn. Neumann was pushed out. SoftBank, which had invested $10 billion in the company at the $47 billion valuation, paid Neumann approximately $1.7 billion to leave.

What makes WeWork specifically useful for this chapter is what it reveals about entitlement operating not as a personality flaw but as an explicit organizational philosophy. Neumann did not conceal the trademark sale, the building leases, or the governance structure. They were in the filing. His apparent position was that the rules that would apply to other founders, the fiduciary obligations, the conflict-of-interest disclosures, the basic separation between a CEO's personal interests and the company's, simply did not apply to him, and that this was not a moral argument he needed to make because it was simply obvious. The rules were for ordinary founders. Adam Neumann was not an ordinary founder.

Bandura's moral disengagement framework identifies 'displacement of responsibility' as one of the key mechanisms: the cognitive move in which personal moral agency is transferred upward or outward, to investors who should have read the filing more carefully, to board members who approved the arrangements, to a market that kept assigning the valuation. WeWork's governance structure made displacement of responsibility into a legal architecture. The ten-to-one voting shares meant that even if every other stakeholder objected, the objection couldn't change anything. Accountability was not merely reduced. It was contractually eliminated.

The $1.7 billion exit package, paid to a founder who had driven the company to the brink of bankruptcy, is the entitlement chapter's most efficient single data point. It is what 'we have the gold, we make the rules' looks like when 'the rules' are written by lawyers and backed by a $10 billion bet that no one wanted to admit had gone wrong.

Entitlement: What It Actually Is and Why It's Not Just Obnoxiousness

The word 'entitlement' in popular usage carries a connotation of mere unpleasantness: the spoiled child, the demanding customer, the executive who expects special treatment. This undersells what the research shows. Entitlement, as a psychological construct, is not just a personality style. It is a cognitive framework that fundamentally reorganizes how a person processes the rules that govern human interaction.

In 2014, Piff published a study in Personality and Social Psychology Bulletin titled 'Wealth and the Inflated Self: Class, Entitlement, and Narcissism.' The findings were not subtle. Wealthier individuals scored significantly higher on measures of narcissism and psychological entitlement. They were more likely to endorse statements indicating they deserve more than others, that rules don't apply to them the way they apply to ordinary people, and that their personal needs should take precedence in social interactions. Crucially, Piff also found that experimentally inducing feelings of egalitarianism, briefly making wealthy participants feel more equal to others, was associated with reductions in these narcissistic tendencies. The entitlement was not fixed. It responded to context. This is important: it means entitlement is a learned and maintained orientation, not an innate trait, which also means it can be unlearned, though the structural conditions of extreme wealth consistently work against that.

Michael Kraus and Dacher Keltner's research program established what they called 'solipsistic social cognition' as a characteristic feature of upper-class psychological orientation. Where lower-class individuals develop what they called 'contextualist' thinking (reading situations carefully, attending to others, understanding outcomes as the product of external factors; upper-class individuals develop thinking organized around the self. Their internal states, goals, and standards become the primary reference point from which external reality is evaluated. This is not arrogance in the colloquial sense. It is a cognitive architecture that places the self at the interpretive center of everything.

The practical output of this architecture is that rules and social constraints are unconsciously filtered through the question: does this rule apply to someone like me? For people who have rarely experienced consequences for violations, who have watched their entire developmental history confirm that money and status provide effective insulation from accountability, the answer that gets encoded is: probably not. And that answer, held confidently enough and confirmed by enough real-world experience, stops feeling like a conclusion. It starts feeling like a fact.

'He was never safe,' Miller told ABC News about Ethan Couch. 'He was bought a toy in Toys 'R' Us when his parents had a fight. In that family, if you hurt someone, send some money.' The family business had multiple run-ins with regulators, multiple settled lawsuits, and a documented pattern of using financial leverage to resolve legal friction. The message delivered to Ethan Couch across sixteen years was not subtle. It was: money resolves consequences. He simply believed it, because it had always been true.

Entitlement is not merely obnoxiousness. It is a cognitive architecture that reorganizes the rules of human interaction around a single organizing principle: those rules are for other people.

Albert Bandura, Moral Disengagement, and How Good People Do Bad Things Without Noticing

Albert Bandura spent sixty-plus years at Stanford building one of the most influential bodies of work in psychology. Most people know him as the architect of social learning theory, the theoretical framework establishing that humans learn behavior by observing and modeling others, not just through direct reinforcement. His work on self-efficacy (the belief in one's own capacity to accomplish goals) shaped everything from therapeutic practice to educational psychology to organizational behavior.

Less known to general audiences but essential to understanding wealthy behavior is his theory of moral disengagement, developed across papers from 1990 onward and synthesized in the 2016 book Moral Disengagement: How People Do Harm and Live with Themselves. The central question Bandura was asking is deceptively simple: how do people who consider themselves decent, moral individuals manage to commit serious harms and feel fine about it afterward?

His answer is that human beings have extraordinarily sophisticated cognitive machinery for neutralizing their own moral standards when those standards would otherwise produce discomfort about their behavior. This machinery, which Bandura identified as a set of eight distinct mechanisms, does not work by changing a person's stated values. It works by constructing a plausible cognitive story about why this particular action, in this particular context, is exempt from those values. The result is that the person can behave in ways that violate everything they claim to believe, suffer no internal conflict, and maintain a fully intact positive self-image.

The eight mechanisms Bandura identified are worth naming explicitly, because each one will be immediately recognizable as a pattern used by wealthy and powerful people with regularity and apparent sincerity:

Moral justification: framing harmful conduct as serving a higher moral purpose. The factory closure that 'protects shareholder value and the long-term health of the company.' The wage suppression that 'keeps us competitive so we can preserve jobs overall.' The environmental damage that 'enables economic development that lifts all boats.' The action is harmful. The framing makes it an ethical obligation.

Euphemistic labeling: sanitizing harmful conduct through language that strips it of its human content. Layoffs become 'workforce reductions' or 'right-sizing.' Wage theft becomes 'compensation structure adjustments.' Catastrophic financial product failures become 'market corrections driven by systemic factors.' The language is not accidental. It is functional; it creates psychological distance between the actor and the human consequences of the action.

Advantageous comparison: making one's harmful conduct appear benign by comparison to something worse. 'At least we're not as bad as our competitors.' 'At least I haven't done what [other executive] did.' 'Compared to the damage caused by [competing industry], our impact is minimal.' The comparison is always selected to make the current behavior look acceptable against the alternative reference point.

Displacement of responsibility: relocating the sense of personal agency onto an authority, a system, or a process. 'I was following fiduciary duty.' 'The board required this.' 'The market made this decision, not me.' 'I didn't write the law, I just operate within it.' This mechanism is extraordinarily well-suited to corporate structures, where chains of accountability can be extended almost indefinitely and any individual actor can position themselves as merely compliant with forces above them.

Diffusion of responsibility: distributing responsibility across so many actors that no one person feels meaningfully accountable. 'Everyone on the committee agreed.' 'This was a collective decision.' 'The whole industry does this.' When responsibility is diffuse, its weight on any individual conscience becomes negligible.

Distortion of consequences: minimizing, ignoring, or doubting the harm one's actions cause. 'There's no real evidence our product causes that.' 'The studies are contested.' 'The effects are exaggerated by activists with an agenda.' This mechanism thrives in contexts like corporate environments, regulatory proceedings, and media ecosystems, where sufficiently resourced parties can generate genuine-looking uncertainty about empirical facts.

Dehumanization: stripping the people affected by one's actions of their full humanity. This mechanism is well-documented in warfare and atrocity contexts, but Bandura documented it operating in everyday corporate and political life as well. Workers become 'human resources' or 'headcount.' Affected communities become 'stakeholders,' a word that technically acknowledges their existence while implying their primary relevance is instrumental. The language of business is, to a significant degree, a continuous exercise in managed dehumanization.

Attribution of blame: making the victim responsible for their own suffering. 'Those employees knew the industry was volatile when they took the jobs.' 'If people can't afford the product at this price, they need to manage their budgets better.' 'The communities affected by this should have diversified their economic base.' This mechanism is particularly powerful because it requires no factual distortion; it simply selects which facts to emphasize in a narrative about causation.

Bandura's key insight is that these mechanisms do not operate sequentially or consciously. They operate as an automatic system of cognitive inoculation, preprocessing potentially troubling actions before they reach the level where internal moral judgment would engage. The person using these mechanisms does not experience themselves as rationalizing. They experience themselves as thinking clearly. The defense is invisible to the person deploying it, which is what makes it so effective and so difficult to challenge from the outside.

Bandura's mechanisms of moral disengagement do not work by changing what people believe is right. They work by constructing a story about why this particular action is exempt from those beliefs, invisibly, automatically, and to the sincere satisfaction of the person doing it.

The Consequence Gap: What Happens to Ethics When Rules Stop Applying

The Ethan Couch case is useful not because it is typical but because it is visible; the mechanism of entitlement-enabled moral disengagement was documented and argued out loud in open court rather than remaining implicit in the ordinary operation of corporate decision-making.

But the structural dynamic it illustrates is not exotic. It is the ordinary condition of people who have experienced sustained immunity from consequences.

Bandura, in his analysis of corporate moral disengagement, was specific about the conditions that enable it: distance from the people harmed, diffusion of responsibility across organizational hierarchies, euphemistic language that obscures the human content of decisions, and, critically, a track record of consequence-free transgression that confirms the person's working theory that the normal rules do not apply to them. Corporate structures provide all of these conditions simultaneously and systematically. They are, in Bandura's description, moral disengagement machines.

The comparison that the Ethan Couch case invites, between the wealthy teenager and his less wealthy contemporary who killed one person with a lower BAC and received twenty years in prison from the same judge, is not a logical argument about legal theory. It is an empirical observation about how the rules actually operate when wealth is and isn't present. The judge, Jean Boyd, did not explain her reasoning publicly. She didn't need to. The different treatment spoke plainly enough.

This differential application of consequences, documented, consistent, and not particularly controversial as an empirical observation, is also, from a psychological standpoint, a learning environment. What is learned, when money reliably reduces consequences, is exactly what Miller described in the Couch household: that wealth buys privilege and there is no rational link between behavior and consequences. This is not a moral failing of the individual who learns this lesson. It is the accurate processing of the available evidence. The lesson is correct. The problem is what happens to ethical reasoning once it has been learned.

Michael Kraus, in an interview about the empathy research, offered a framing that applies equally to the entitlement problem: 'Particularly with how capitalism structures society, being really rich requires a measure of not caring about someone else. Maybe it is the warehouse worker fulfilling Christmas shipping orders or communities in Africa devastated by the mining of cobalt and other raw materials for batteries that we use for electric vehicles. To accumulate wealth requires paying less attention to the suffering experienced by those that are exploited by that accumulation.'

This is not a radical critique. It is a description of structural incentives. The system rewards not-caring. Not-caring is further enabled by moral disengagement mechanisms that make it cognitively comfortable. The result is a population at the top of the income distribution that has been systematically trained, over years of consequence-free transgression and comfortable rationalization, to feel entirely at ease with behavior that causes serious harm to others.

What Accountability Actually Requires

The instinctive response to all of this is to conclude that wealthy people need to be better people, to develop more empathy, more conscience, more willingness to hold themselves accountable. This response is understandable, psychologically naive, and functionally useless.

Bandura's most important practical conclusion, after identifying all the mechanisms of moral disengagement, was that personal ethical standards are insufficient safeguards against them. In his 1999 paper, he wrote: 'Civilized life requires, in addition to humane personal standards, safeguards built into social systems that uphold compassionate behavior and renounce cruelty.' The key word is 'requires.' Not 'would benefit from.' Requires.

His reasoning is straightforward: moral disengagement is not a disorder or a failure of character. It is a normal cognitive capacity that operates in all human beings under the right conditions. The conditions that activate it are: distance from consequences, diffusion of responsibility, available rationalizations, and absence of external accountability. Concentrated wealth reliably provides all four. The solution is not to ask people to override a hardwired psychological tendency through willpower and good intentions. The solution is to restructure the conditions that activate the tendency.

What that restructuring looks like in practice is Chapter Eleven's territory. But the conceptual point that Bandura established, and that the research in this and every preceding chapter supports, is that voluntary ethics do not work as a primary safeguard when structural conditions consistently reward their suspension. This is not a counsel of despair. It is a design specification. Systems that require voluntary good behavior from people whose entire structural reality tells them they are exempt from normal rules are systems that have been designed to fail.

The Ethan Couch case produced national outrage. It also produced the normal follow-on: media coverage, public debate, and then the same judge continuing to apply the same differential standards to other defendants in subsequent cases, because the structural incentives that produced the original decision remained intact. Outrage, it turns out, is not accountability. It is the feeling people have when they can see the mechanism clearly but lack the structural tools to change it.

Understanding the mechanism is the first step toward the tools. We now understand the mechanism. Dopamine loops that make wealth neurologically addictive. Mirror neuron suppression and empathy erosion that make other people's suffering progressively less legible. Hubris syndrome that deteriorates judgment at the top of the power curve. Corporate psychopathy structures that filter for and reward the absence of conscience. Consistent historical patterns confirming that this is not a bug or an era-specific anomaly. Documented empathy deficits across multiple physiological measures. And now: the specific cognitive architecture, entitlement and moral disengagement, through which all of the above finds practical expression in decisions that harm millions of people while the decision-makers sleep soundly.

That is a fairly complete account of how wealthy people got the way they are. The next question is what they do with it. Which, unfortunately, involves sex.

The rules are not decorative for most people. They are encoded in the feedback loops: consequences, social disapproval, the simple experience of having to live inside the outcomes of your choices, that make ethical behavior feel necessary rather than optional. When those feedback loops are systematically disconnected by wealth and power, what remains is not immorality exactly. It is a cognitive architecture that has simply been relieved of the inputs that morality runs on. Stage Five of the Cycle is complete. Stage Six, System Capture, is where it becomes everyone else's problem.

Chapter 8

Sex, Power, and Why This Keeps Happening

Spoiler: it's not about attraction. It's about dominance. It's always been about dominance.

On October 5, 2017, The New York Times published a story about Harvey Weinstein.

Within days, dozens of women had come forward. Within weeks, the count was over eighty. Actresses, assistants, aspiring filmmakers, hotel employees: the range was not the range of a man with a type. It was the range of a man who had treated proximity to power as a hunting condition. The industry he worked in was merely the particular territory where he had accumulated enough institutional control to make the behavior sustainable for decades.

What made the Weinstein story different from a celebrity scandal was what emerged about the infrastructure around it. This was not a secret kept by one man. It was a secret kept by an entire ecosystem: agents who knew and said nothing, executives who heard rumors and looked away, journalists who reported and had the stories killed, lawyers whose specific professional function was the construction of legal instruments: nondisclosure agreements, settlement arrangements, and retaliatory threats, designed to ensure that any woman who reported the behavior would find the machinery of an industry arrayed against her credibility. Weinstein had not simply committed acts. He had built a system for committing them indefinitely.

When he was convicted in 2020, the response in some quarters was to treat the verdict as a resolution, as proof that the system had worked, that accountability was possible, that the reckoning had arrived. But within three years, similar structures had been documented in film, television, music, venture capital, politics, professional sports, medicine, academia, and organized religion. Not copy-cat behavior inspired by Weinstein's notoriety. Pre-existing systems, suddenly visible in the new light.

The collective response to each new revelation follows a script so well-rehearsed it practically performs itself. Shock. Outrage. Think pieces. More accusers. Denials that downgrade to 'I'm sorry if anyone was made to feel uncomfortable.' Resignation or firing or, in a meaningful minority of cases, criminal charges. Then a period of institutional soul-searching, new policies, and the quiet return of the next iteration of the same dynamic.

If this were about individual monsters, aberrant bad actors whose presence in institutions is bad luck, the pattern would be random. Predators would appear across the income and power distribution with equal frequency. They don't. Which means the monster theory is wrong. And if the monster theory is wrong, the solution of removing individual monsters cannot be right.

This chapter is about what is actually happening.

Lather. Rinse. Repeat.

In February 2017, a software engineer named Susan Fowler published a blog post.

It was approximately 3,000 words long. It described, in precise and specific detail, her experience as an engineer at Uber: a manager who propositioned her on her first official day on the team, HR's response when she reported it (the manager was 'a high performer' and this was 'his first offense,' so no action would be taken), subsequent retaliation when she continued to raise concerns, a pattern she discovered through informal conversations with other women that suggested the 'first offense' claim was false, and a year-long experience of watching the company's stated commitment to diversity function as performance rather than policy.

Within a week, Uber's board had retained former Attorney General Eric Holder to conduct an investigation. Within six months, the investigation had produced a 13-point reform agenda, the head of HR had resigned, and Travis Kalanick had been forced out as CEO. A subsequent shareholder lawsuit alleged that the board had known about harassment complaints and done nothing. Kalanick settled with investors for $245 million.

Fowler's account became a catalyst for what would become, eight months later, the broader #MeToo moment, not because it was unique, but because it was so precisely documented. She had kept records. She had the email chains. She could establish a timeline. In an environment designed to prevent exactly that kind of documentation (the informal conversation, the 'first offense' framing, the HR process that produced no paper trail), Fowler had created paper anyway.

The Uber case is instructive for this chapter because it maps the institutional infrastructure of impunity with unusual clarity. The manager who propositioned Fowler was not acting without organizational context. He was acting inside an organization that had communicated, through its promotion patterns, its stated tolerance for 'brilliant jerks,' and its HR function's actual behavior versus its stated policies, that certain behaviors were not career-limiting for high performers. The 'first offense' framing was not an isolated HR error. It was a policy, a standard response that distributed across enough cases to constitute an institutional position.

Kalanick's own behavior during this period, documented in Uber board meeting recordings, in his famous video argument with an Uber driver that went viral in February 2017, and in the Holder investigation's findings, illustrates the power-disinhibition dynamic from Chapter Two in its fully developed form. He had built an organization explicitly modeled on his own psychological profile. The culture was not an accident. It was a reflection. When the organization's behavior became publicly indefensible, the board's response was to remove the reflection, not to examine what had built it.

Susan Fowler's blog post did not expose a bad actor. It exposed a system that had been operating as designed. The system's design was the problem. The individual was just the part they could remove.

If this were about individual monsters, aberrant bad actors whose presence in institutions is a matter of bad luck rather than structural logic, the pattern would be random. Predators would appear across the income distribution with roughly equal frequency. Their behavior would not cluster in industries and organizations where power differentials are steepest. Victims would report at similar rates regardless of the economic stakes. Institutions would investigate with equal vigor regardless of who was implicated.

None of those things are true. Which means the monster theory is wrong.

This chapter is about what is actually happening. Not the individual case (those are documented extensively and don't require rehearsal here), but the psychological and structural mechanism that produces the pattern. Because there is a mechanism. It has been studied. It is understood. And understanding it turns out to be far less comfortable than the monster theory, because the monster theory lets institutions off the hook. The mechanism does not.

Every few years we're shocked, genuinely shocked, that a powerful man abused that power. At some point, shocked has to become prepared.

The Power-Sex Link: It's Wired, Not Chosen

In 1995, social psychologist John Bargh and colleagues published a study in the Journal of Personality and Social Psychology with a title so clinical it almost hides what it's saying: 'Attractiveness of the Underling: An Automatic Power-Sex Association and Its Consequences for

Sexual Harassment.' The operative word is automatic.

Bargh and his team were testing whether the cognitive association between power and sex (the mental link between holding authority over someone and sexual interest in them) operated at the level of automatic, preconscious processing or only emerged as a deliberate, conscious thought. This matters enormously. Deliberate cognition is suppressible. Automatic cognition is not. It happens before the person decides anything. It happens, in fact, before the person knows it's happening.

The results were unambiguous. Men primed to think about power showed faster automatic activation of sexual concepts than men primed with neutral material. The power prime didn't make them think consciously about sex; it activated the association below the threshold of awareness. The hierarchical relationship itself, the cognitive framework of having authority over a person, was neurologically linked to sexual ideation in a way that bypassed deliberate reasoning entirely.

This finding sits at the intersection of two independent research programs, one on power's neurological effects and one on sexual coercion, and connects them in a way that is both scientifically precise and, if you sit with it, genuinely disturbing. It means the problem isn't primarily that some powerful men choose to use their power for sexual access. It means the neurological architecture of power, as we've built it into our institutions, creates an automatic association that must be actively suppressed by anyone who holds it. And as the previous six chapters have established in considerable detail, wealthy and powerful people's capacity for active suppression of their own impulses has been systematically eroded by the same conditions that gave them the power in the first place.

Keltner, who has spent twenty-five years studying what power does to the people who hold it, put the connection explicitly in a 2017 Harvard Business Review piece written in direct response to the Harvey Weinstein exposé: 'In experiments in which one group of people is randomly assigned to a condition of power, people in the powerful group are prone to two shortcomings: They develop empathy deficits and are less able to read others' emotions and take others' perspectives. And they behave in an impulsive fashion; they violate the ethics of the workplace.'

Empathy deficits. Impulsivity. Ethics violations. These are not descriptions of monsters. They are descriptions of the documented neurological effects of holding power over other people. Keltner's framing is important: he explicitly uses the phrase 'banality of the abuses of power,' a deliberate echo of Hannah Arendt's 'banality of evil,' to make the point that the capacity for predatory behavior does not require extraordinary malevolence. It requires ordinary people in extraordinary power differentials.

The question is not who these men are. The question is what power does to whoever holds it.

Disinhibition, Hypocrisy, and the Entitlement-Infidelity Connection

Joris Lammers at Tilburg University in the Netherlands has produced what is arguably the most rigorous body of empirical work on the specific intersection of power, ethics, and sexual behavior. His findings, across multiple studies and collaborators including Adam Galinsky at Northwestern, are worth examining carefully because they close off a set of popular explanations that turn out to be wrong.

In 2011, Lammers and colleagues published in Psychological Science a study that surveyed 1,561 professionals across a range of industries and organizational levels. The headline finding, that elevated power is positively associated with infidelity, was not surprising to anyone who had been paying attention to the news. The mechanism behind the finding was more illuminating. The study found that the relationship between power and infidelity was mediated by confidence in the ability to attract partners. Power increases infidelity, the data showed, because it increases self-perceived attractiveness and desirability. The powerful person believes, with sincere conviction, that their interest will be welcomed. They are not always wrong. But they are wrong far more often than their confidence reflects, and crucially, the confidence exists independent of actual reciprocal interest.

What Lammers and colleagues also found, and what tends to get less attention: the relationship between power and infidelity was identical for women as for men. The common assumption, that male executives cheat at higher rates than female executives because men are constitutionally more prone to it, turned out to be a reflection not of sex but of who historically held power. When women hold equivalent organizational positions, the power-infidelity association is equivalent. This is a finding with significant implications. It means the problem is not testosterone. It is not some specifically male psychological defect. It is power itself, operating through the same mechanisms in whoever holds it.

In a subsequent 2015 study in the Journal of Sex Research, Lammers and Maner found something even more specific: power's relationship with infidelity was statistically mediated by attraction to the counternormative aspect of infidelity, the secrecy, the rule-breaking, the transgression of the social boundary itself. Power doesn't just increase desire for more partners. It increases attraction to the fact that taking them violates a rule. This connects directly back to the disinhibition research from Chapter 2. Power removes the felt weight of constraints. And once constraints feel weightless, transgressing them starts to feel not wrong but exciting.

The 2010 hypocrisy study by Lammers, Stapel, and Galinsky in Psychological Science is the piece that should be on the wall of every HR department in every organization on earth. The study ran five experiments testing a deceptively simple proposition: do powerful people hold themselves to the same moral standards they apply to others? The answer, across all five experiments, was unambiguous. The powerful condemned others' cheating more severely than the less powerful. They also cheated more themselves. They applied stricter moral judgments to others' behavior. They applied looser standards to their own. They experienced no cognitive dissonance about this, which is the most remarkable part. They were not aware they were being hypocritical. The stricter standard for others and the laxer standard for self coexisted without any apparent internal friction.

The final study in that series found something that complicates the narrative usefully: when power was experienced as illegitimate, when participants felt they hadn't really earned it, the hypocrisy effect reversed. The illegitimately powerful actually became stricter with themselves than with others, as if compensating for the unearned position. This matters because it identifies a potential structural lever: the perception of legitimacy. Power that is earned through demonstrable merit, held accountably, and subject to meaningful challenge operates differently on the person who holds it than power that is inherited, accumulated through extraction, or maintained through institutional protection. The latter is precisely the condition that concentrated wealth creates.

The powerful condemned others' cheating more severely. They also cheated more themselves. They experienced no cognitive dissonance about this, which is the most remarkable part.

The Infrastructure of Silence: How Institutions Protect the Pattern

None of what the research describes (the automatic power-sex association, the disinhibition of impulse control, the hypocrisy dynamic, the infidelity confidence) would produce the scale of documented harm without an institutional infrastructure that converts individual predatory behavior into an ongoing system.

That infrastructure has a primary mechanism: the non-disclosure agreement.

An NDA, in its legitimate use, protects trade secrets and proprietary business information. In its application to sexual misconduct settlements, it does something functionally different: it converts a pattern of harm into a series of isolated, confidential incidents, each resolved quietly with money, each legally sealed from the next. The perpetrator's record before any new victim, any new employer, any new institutional context appears clean. The institutional memory of the pattern is erased, replaced by a series of financial entries categorized as confidential legal settlements.

The scale of NDA use in American workplaces is not trivial. Research published in the Vanderbilt Law Review found that roughly one in three American workers is bound by a non-disclosure agreement of some kind. The concentration of NDA use in settlements involving power differentials, where the powerful party can fund aggressive legal action and the less powerful party cannot, means the instrument functions, in practice, as a wealth-powered silencing technology.

The Stanford Clayman Institute for Gender Research and advocacy group Lift Our Voices released a 2024 report documenting the experience of twenty-three employees who had signed NDAs in workplace misconduct cases. The accounts were consistent in their structure: vague and broad language that left employees uncertain about their own rights; company lawyers who exploited that ambiguity to pressure rapid settlement; and provisions so sweeping that signatories could not discuss what had happened with family members, therapists, or personal attorneys. One participant's account captures the dynamic with precision: 'I wanted to speak out. And I was reminded: I had signed an NDA and not to speak, not to disclose what happened. I was already down. I was already devastated.'

The Clayman report's central finding was not just that NDAs silenced individual victims; it also shielded perpetrators and prevented institutions from identifying or addressing patterns. You cannot solve a problem that has been legally erased. Each new incident arrives in an institutional context with no documented history, reviewed by HR professionals who have no access to the sealed settlements, assessed by leadership with genuine plausible deniability about what their colleague has done before. The NDA doesn't just protect the individual perpetrator. It protects the institution's ability to believe its own PR.

Zelda Perkins, Harvey Weinstein's former assistant, signed an NDA in 1998 that prevented her from speaking about his behavior for nearly twenty years. When she finally broke it in 2017, accepting the legal risk to do so, she described the settlement process as one in which she had no real choice, no real legal leverage, and no real protection. 'There is no justice for women,' she said. 'The only thing that I can do is make it a business liability for them to keep NDAs.'

Her framing is exactly correct, and it is exactly the framing the research supports: the only thing that produces behavioral change in institutions is altering the cost-benefit calculation. Not moral argument. Not policy statements. Not annual harassment training delivered via mandatory e-learning modules that everyone clicks through in eight minutes. Changed financial incentives. When protecting a serial predator becomes more expensive than removing him, institutions remove him. Until then, they protect him. This is not cynicism. It is an accurate description of institutional decision-making under the conditions that concentrated power creates.

Why Victims Don't Report, and What Would Actually Change That

The question that appears in every discussion of workplace sexual misconduct (why didn't they report sooner?) has an answer so well-documented that asking it as a genuine inquiry, in 2026, requires either willful ignorance or the specific kind of motivated reasoning that we have now spent six chapters naming.

People don't report because the reporting system is controlled by the institution that employs both them and the person they would be reporting. Because the financial and career consequences of reporting are asymmetric, borne almost entirely by the person with less power. Because the research on witness behavior in hierarchical organizations shows consistently that bystanders in elite environments face specific barriers to intervention: the higher the status of the perpetrator, the lower the perceived probability that intervention will produce any outcome other than retaliation. Because the person in the position to take action is typically someone whose career advancement depends on the goodwill of the person being accused.

This is the organizational bystander effect operating in a power-concentrated environment. The classic bystander research by Darley and Latané's foundational work from the 1960s establishing that the presence of others reduces individual intervention, has been extensively extended to organizational contexts. In elite organizations, the relevant dynamic is not the diffusion of responsibility across equals (the standard bystander model) but the suppression of intervention by people who understand, with perfect accuracy, that speaking up about a senior person's behavior will primarily damage themselves.

Keltner's institutional analysis in the 2017 HBR piece identifies the specific organizational features that sustain predatory behavior: isolation of the perpetrator from feedback, subordinates who are financially dependent on the perpetrator's goodwill, HR systems that function as instruments of institutional reputation management rather than victim protection, and boards that are selected partly for loyalty to senior leadership and thus have a structural bias toward believing what senior leadership tells them. These are not design flaws in otherwise functional institutions. In many cases, they are design features, structures that emerged precisely because they protected the revenue-generating capacity of high-status individuals.

What would actually change things is structurally distinct from what institutions announce when the pressure gets acute. Anonymous reporting systems help, but only when the anonymity is credible and the receiving end is genuinely independent of institutional leadership, conditions rarely met. Mandatory training helps at the margins for people who are ambivalent, not for people who are predatory. Mandatory reporting requirements with genuine teeth (legal obligation, third-party investigation, enforceable penalties, and NDA restrictions that prevent pattern erasure) have measurable effects, because they change the cost-benefit calculation.

The 2018 California law banning NDA provisions in settlements involving sexual harassment and discrimination claims is the most concrete structural example of what effective policy looks like: it removes one primary tool of the infrastructure of silence, creating conditions where institutional pattern recognition becomes possible. Legislative action at the federal level, specifically the Congressional Accountability and Hush Fund Elimination Act prohibiting NDA requirements in federal government sexual misconduct procedures, represents the same logic applied to a different institutional context.

The common thread is not culture change through awareness. Culture changes when incentives change. Incentives change when laws change.

Laws change when the political will to enact them exceeds the political and financial power of the institutions that benefit from the status quo. The previous chapter established that those institutions have a great deal of political and financial power. This chapter has established that they use it, in part, to protect the conditions under which their most powerful members operate with impunity.

That is the loop. The wealth creates the power. The power creates the disinhibition. The disinhibition creates the behavior. The institutional protection (legal, financial, and reputational) creates the silence. The silence creates the conditions for the next iteration. And every few years, when enough people break enough NDAs at the same time, we are shocked again.

At some point, shocked has to become prepared.

The research suggests exactly what preparation looks like: not better individuals at the top of the hierarchy, but better structural constraints on what anyone at the top of the hierarchy can do without accountability. The focus on individual character is not just insufficient. It is a deliberate misdirection that serves the infrastructure it purports to address. The monster theory protects the system. The structural theory threatens it. This is not a coincidence.

Next chapter: we talk about what happens when wealthy people decide to fix all of this through the power of charitable giving. Brace yourself.

Power over resources and power over bodies operate through the same underlying psychology:

the reduction of accountability, the elimination of meaningful consequences, the institutional capture of the systems that might otherwise intervene. The Cycle's Stage Five extends into domains that most analyses of wealth psychology avoid. Stage Six, System Capture, is where the individual dynamics of the first five stages become infrastructure.

Chapter 9

The Philanthropy Con

Buying Goodness at Wholesale Prices

They'll donate a library named after themselves before they'll pay their employees a living wage.

There is a hospital wing in this country (in many cities, actually) with a name on the wall. A family name, usually. Engraved in something expensive. Lit from below. The wing was funded by a donation. The donation was tax-deductible. The family whose name is on the wall also runs a company that, in the same year the donation was made, reduced its employee health insurance contribution to lower operating costs.

This is not a hypothetical. It is a pattern so common that it has ceased to register as irony and has settled into the comfortable furniture of normal institutional life. The naming rights to a hospital wing cost approximately five million dollars. Restoring the health insurance contribution would have cost roughly three million. One of these purchases comes with a plaque and a tax deduction. The other is just an expense.

This is the philanthropy chapter. It is going to make some people uncomfortable, because the critique of billionaire charity sounds, at first pass, like the argument of someone who doesn't want rich people to give away money. That is not the argument. The argument is considerably more specific than that, and it requires distinguishing between two things that look identical from the outside but function very differently: charity that costs the giver something, and charity that costs the giver nothing, or, in many cases, actually turns a profit.

The Sackler family, owners of Purdue Pharma, were for decades among the most celebrated philanthropists in the world. Their name graced galleries at the Metropolitan Museum of Art, the Louvre, the Tate Modern, the Guggenheim, the Smithsonian, the Victoria and Albert Museum, and scores of academic institutions. They were giving away significant money. They were also, through Purdue Pharma's aggressive marketing of OxyContin, materially contributing to an opioid epidemic that killed hundreds of thousands of Americans. The galleries received the donations. The families of the dead received nothing. The Sackler name was synonymous with generosity for decades, right up until it became synonymous with something else.

Anand Giridharadas, in his 2018 book Winners Take All: The Elite Charade of Changing the World, describes this dynamic with a phrase that is difficult to improve upon: philanthropists behaving like 'arsonists as firefighters.' They fund the solutions to problems they also fund the creation of. And they receive cultural credit for the firefighting without paying any cultural cost for the arson.

Naming rights to a hospital wing cost $5 million. Restoring the employee health insurance contribution would have cost $3 million. One comes with a plaque and a tax deduction. The other is just an expense.

The Psychology First: Moral Licensing and the Charity Permission Slip

Before getting to the financial mechanics, which are genuinely alarming and deserve their own section, it is worth establishing the psychological foundation, because the financial structure didn't arise from nowhere. It arose from a particular psychological dynamic that the research documents with considerable precision.

Moral licensing is the name for what happens, cognitively and behaviorally, when a person performs a virtuous act and subsequently uses the psychological credit from that act to permit less virtuous behavior. It was studied systematically by Anna Merritt, Daniel Effron, and Benoît Monin at Stanford, with their 2010 paper 'Moral Self-Licensing: When Being Good Frees Us to Be Bad' serving as the field's foundational review. The mechanism is simple: doing good produces a psychological surplus, a sense of moral credit. That credit then reduces the internal resistance to behaviors that would otherwise trigger guilt or self-condemnation. The person experiences not 'I'm about to do something bad' but 'I've earned the right to do this.'

The research demonstrating this effect is extensive and, once you start looking for it, recognizable everywhere. People who shopped in eco-friendly stores were more likely to cheat and steal in subsequent tasks than people who shopped in conventional stores (Mazar and Zhong, 2010).

Participants who established their non-racist credentials in one scenario were more willing to make potentially prejudiced decisions in the next one (Monin and Miller, 2001). Consumers who planned to donate to charity were more than twice as likely to choose luxury goods over practical purchases in a subsequent shopping scenario, and the planning alone was sufficient; they didn't even have to actually donate. You can license yourself for future misbehavior by merely intending to be good.

That last finding is the one that should be stapled to every philanthropic foundation's annual report: even the intention to give triggers moral licensing before a single dollar changes hands. The billionaire who announces a ten-billion-dollar pledge to global health and then spends the next fiscal year lobbying against pharmaceutical price regulation is not being incoherently hypocritical. He is operating, with neurological precision, exactly as the moral licensing research would predict. The pledge established the credential. The credential licensed the lobbying. The internal ledger balanced. He feels fine.

global health then lobbies against pharmaceutical price regulation.' (end of 'The Psychology First' section, before 'The Financial

The pledge economy, the ecosystem of announced charitable commitments, multi-decade giving promises, and DAF contributions that dominate elite philanthropic discourse, has a specific psychological feature that the moral licensing research illuminates clearly: most of it never actually has to happen. The Giving Pledge, the initiative launched in 2010 by Bill Gates and Warren Buffett through which billionaires commit to giving the majority of their wealth to philanthropy, is legally unenforceable. It is a public commitment, not a binding contract. Several early signatories have died without fulfilling their pledges. The pledge establishes the moral credential, and the credential is what does the psychological work, regardless of whether the money moves.

This is not primarily an accusation of bad faith. It is a description of a system that has been designed, whether intentionally or through accumulated incentive structures, to maximize credential production relative to actual wealth transfer. A billion-dollar pledge announced at a press conference produces more reputational benefit (in terms of media coverage, social status, and the regulatory goodwill that reduces scrutiny of the underlying business operations) than a hundred million dollars quietly transferred to a community foundation that funds structural change. The pledge economy rewards the announcement. The actual charitable sector, and the communities it serves, needs the money.

There is a more uncomfortable extension of moral licensing that Merritt and colleagues documented: moral credentials don't just license future misbehavior. They license present misbehavior by reinterpreting it. When a person has established strong moral credentials, as in a philanthropist's case with a decades-long public record of charitable giving, subsequent harmful behavior is interpreted through that credential. The harm is minimized, contextualized, attributed to circumstances rather than character, viewed as an exception rather than a pattern. Observers extend the benefit of the doubt proportional to the credit balance. The Sackler galleries weren't just a PR strategy, in other words. They were a cognitive inoculation system, building a credential reserve that would, for decades, make the harmful behavior harder for observers, and probably for the Sacklers themselves, to see clearly.

Merritt and colleagues also documented what they called the 'strategic pursuit of moral credentials,' evidence that people proactively establish moral credentials before engaging in behavior they already anticipate will be morally questionable. They're not licensing after the fact. They're pre-loading the permission slip. A company that announces a major philanthropic commitment shortly before a regulatory hearing, a labor dispute, or a product liability settlement is not being coincidentally generous. It is executing, with whatever degree of conscious awareness, a well-documented psychological strategy.

The Financial Architecture: How 'Giving Away' Money Isn't

Set the psychology aside for a moment and look at the math, because the math is genuinely instructive.

When a very wealthy person donates appreciated stock to a charitable vehicle, specifically stock that has grown significantly in value since it was purchased, two things happen simultaneously. They receive an immediate income tax deduction for the full current market value of the stock. And they avoid paying capital gains tax on the appreciation. If the stock was purchased for ten thousand dollars and is now worth one hundred thousand, the donor deducts one hundred thousand from their taxable income and pays zero tax on the ninety thousand dollars of gain. A non-wealthy person who liquidated the same asset and donated the proceeds would pay capital gains tax first, have less money to donate, and receive a smaller deduction. The tax code, in this specific construction, is literally more generous to people who have more. This is not controversial as a factual description. It is simply how the system works.

The donor-advised fund (the DAF) takes this structure and adds a layer that converts the timing advantage into something more durable. A DAF is, in basic terms, a charitable account into which donors make tax-deductible contributions and from which they can recommend grants to operating charities at their discretion, on their timeline, subject to no mandatory payout schedule. The immediate tax benefit is locked in at contribution. The actual distribution to working charities is optional, delayed, and potentially indefinite.

By the end of 2022, DAFs held nearly $230 billion in assets. In 2022 alone, DAFs distributed approximately $52 billion to charities, which sounds substantial until you note that roughly $86 billion was contributed in the same year. The gap between contributions and distributions is not a rounding error. It is a structural feature. And in a study of more than 2,600 DAF accounts by the Council of Michigan Foundations, the majority of donors paid out less than 5 percent of assets in a given year. More than one-third gave nothing to charity at all in that year, while sitting on tax-deducted funds.

The Nonprofit Quarterly's analysis of this structure cuts directly to the accountability gap: the 'wealth defense industry,' the lawyers, accountants, and financial managers who maximize assets and minimize taxes for wealthy clients, has enthusiastically embraced DAFs not primarily as charitable vehicles but as tools for tax-advantaged dynastic wealth retention. Donors can offload hard-to-value assets to maximize deductions. DAF accounts can provide anonymity, enabling funds to reach political causes and even, as documented, hate groups, with no public disclosure. Private foundation donors can use DAFs to satisfy payout requirements without money reaching operating charities. And roughly $2.5 billion annually cycles among DAF sponsors, money moving from one charitable account to another, counting as charitable distributions without actually reaching any organization doing anything.

What this means in practice is that the tax deduction, which is funded by other taxpayers who must make up for the lost public revenue, often precedes actual charitable activity by years or decades, if it arrives at all. Public money is subsidizing private philanthropic intent, and the public has no mechanism to verify when or whether that intent materializes into benefit.

The tax deduction is immediate. The charitable obligation is optional. The gap between those two facts is measured in billions of dollars annually and funded by everyone who pays taxes.

Giridharadas and the Win-Win Trap

Anand Giridharadas spent several years inside the world he eventually wrote about. He was awarded a Henry Crown Fellowship at the Aspen Institute in 2011, participated in gatherings at Davos and the Clinton Global Initiative, flew in private jets with entrepreneurial leaders who were earnestly committed to improving the world. His criticism in Winners Take All, published in 2018 and still, seven years later, essentially confirmed by subsequent events, is not the criticism of an outside agitator lobbing accusations. It is the testimony of an insider who took seriously what was being said and then looked hard at what was actually happening.

His central argument is encapsulated in the phrase 'win-win.' The philanthropic and social change sector in his account has been colonized by a logic that requires any acceptable solution to inequality or social harm to also be profitable, or at minimum revenue-neutral, for the people at the top of the system that produced the problem. 'Social change that offers a kickback to the winners is favored,' he argues, 'and forms of social change that don't are not.'

The implication is structurally significant: this framework excludes, by design, the interventions most likely to be effective. Raising minimum wages is not a win-win for employers. Universal healthcare is not a win-win for insurance companies. Progressive taxation is not a win-win for people whose taxes would increase. Strong labor protections are not a win-win for shareholders whose dividends depend on wage suppression. The specific solutions that would most directly address the conditions producing the inequality that philanthropists claim to be addressing are precisely the solutions that the win-win framework rules out of acceptable consideration.

'Many believe they are changing the world when they may instead, or also, be protecting a system that is at the root of the problems they wish to solve,' Giridharadas writes. 'Business elites are taking over the work of changing the world.' He profiles a former Facebook employee who wanted to help gig workers navigate income instability. She built a phone app. For $260 a year, it would help workers manage their irregular income. This is the philanthropic-entrepreneurial ecosystem's preferred solution to a problem whose actual cause is the legal structure that classifies those workers as contractors rather than employees, removes their eligibility for benefits, and eliminates their legal right to organize. The app helps workers cope. It does not address what produces the condition requiring coping.

Giridharadas quotes charity leaders off the record in terms that are striking: after receiving funding from major philanthropic institutions, they were made to understand that they should stop using the word 'inequality' in their public communications and substitute 'opportunity.' The word change is not cosmetic. 'Inequality' implies a structural problem with a structural cause, requiring structural remediation. 'Opportunity' implies individual deficits addressable through individual intervention. One of these framings threatens the donors. The other doesn't. The funded organizations adopted the safer framing. Their funders' constraints on acceptable language are not written into grant agreements. They don't need to be. Everyone understands how the game works.

By 2025, Giridharadas had concluded that recent years proved his argument more thoroughly than the book itself had. 'I want to thank the billionaire class for making a case for what I was trying to argue much better than I ever could,' he told Time magazine. 'Elon Musk, Mark Zuckerberg, Jeff Bezos, et cetera, have staged a play in public for why this level of wealth is dangerous.'

What Actual Accountability Looks Like, and How to Spot the Real Thing

None of this means that all philanthropy is a con. Some of it is genuinely costly to the donor, genuinely effective in its impact, and genuinely free of the control-and-credential dynamics this chapter has described. The problem is that those cases are indistinguishable at a surface level from the much larger category of philanthropy-as-reputation-management. Both come with press releases, foundation websites, Aspen Institute appearances, and TED talks about changing the world.

There are a small number of signals that distinguish them, and it is worth naming them directly.

The first signal is whether the giving addresses the causes of the problems the donor benefits from, or only the symptoms. A technology billionaire who funds coding bootcamps for unemployed workers is addressing a symptom. One who supports labor organizing, antitrust enforcement, or universal basic income is addressing a cause, and paying a cost, because those solutions directly threaten their own business model. The latter category is rare. Its rarity is itself informative.

The second signal is whether the giving involves democratic accountability or private control. Taxes flow into public systems where elected officials, subject to public pressure, determine allocations. Private foundations and DAFs flow into whatever the donor decides to fund, subject to no democratic input and minimal public accountability. Giridharadas's argument is not that taxes are administered well (they often aren't), but that they are administered democratically, with the possibility of accountability through political processes that philanthropy structurally forecloses. A billionaire who funds a school system gets to determine educational priorities. A billionaire who pays taxes and advocates for school funding through public budgets does not. The difference in democratic legitimacy is not subtle.

The third signal, and the one that requires the most careful observation, is the ratio of advocacy to donation. A philanthropist who gives substantially and also advocates publicly for the systemic changes that would make their giving unnecessary is performing a fundamentally different act than one who gives substantially and simultaneously lobbies against the regulations that would produce those changes at scale. The second billionaire is buying silence, reputation insurance, and the continued gratitude of institutions that depend on their continuing to exist. That's not charity. That's a subscription.

The fourth signal is anonymity. Philanthropy that requires no public disclosure, flowing through donor-advised funds with the sponsor listed rather than the donor, is philanthropy that seeks the moral credit without the accountability. You cannot assess the ratio of giving to harm, the relationship between stated values and actual funding, or the proportion of donated-versus-retained wealth from a transaction that is legally sealed. Meaningful accountability requires transparency. Anonymity is, by definition, its opposite.

The reader who walks away from this chapter with a more skeptical eye toward the philanthropist's press release, who thinks to ask, before joining the applause, what percentage of the company's workforce is uninsured, what the CEO's pay ratio to median worker looks like, what regulatory battles the foundation donor fought in the same quarter the donation was announced, is the reader this chapter was written for. The plaque is always more visible than the balance sheet. The applause is always louder than the fine print.

Understanding this doesn't require cynicism about human generosity in general. Humans are genuinely generous. The research on prosocial behavior is robust and heartening. The specific pattern described in this chapter is not a claim about human nature; it is a claim about what happens to a specific subset of humans when they accumulate enough wealth to purchase moral reputation at scale, insulate themselves from consequences, and operate in environments that reinforce the story they want to believe about themselves.

The next chapter asks what happens when that pattern compounds across generations. Spoiler: it gets weirder.

The Wealth Insanity Cycle completes its loop not with an individual going visibly off the rails, but with an institution (philanthropy, in this case) being quietly reorganized to serve the cycle's continuation rather than interrupt it. Donor-advised funds are not a bug. They are Stage Six operating as designed: a system that converts individual moral disengagement into structural advantage, taxed by the public, directed by the donor, accountable to no one. The next chapter examines how the Cycle transmits itself across generations, which is where it gets genuinely strange.

Chapter 10

Inherited Crazy

Dynastic Wealth and the Psychology of People Who Never Had to Earn It

Old money is new money that's been sitting in a dark room for three generations getting weird.

Somewhere in Connecticut, a twenty-six-year-old is having a very bad Tuesday.

He is not having a bad Tuesday because he lacks resources. He has resources in a quantity that would be difficult to spend in several lifetimes at normal human consumption rates. He is having a bad Tuesday because his trust administrator has declined to authorize a wire transfer he requested, on the grounds that the trust's terms require co-trustee approval for transfers above a certain threshold, and the co-trustee, an uncle with whom relations are complicated, has not responded to emails. He is therefore having to call his lawyer. This is the third time this month he has had to call his lawyer about something his father would have simply handled.

His father, the one who built the company, whose portrait hangs in the foyer and whose face appears on a hospital wing in a city he visited three times, would have known how to handle it. His father understood money in the way that people who have made money understand it: as a thing that responds to decisions, that moves in directions you choose, that can be lost and therefore must be respected. His father woke up at 5 AM for thirty years because he knew, in a way that lived in his body, what happened when you didn't.

The twenty-six-year-old does not have this knowledge. He has never needed it. The money was simply there, structured around him like the architecture of a building: present, load-bearing, and entirely designed by someone else. He did not build it and he does not fully understand it and this particular Tuesday it is not doing what he told it to do, which is infuriating, because things are supposed to do what he tells them.

There is a saying, old enough that it has been attributed to Andrew Carnegie, that goes: shirtsleeves to shirtsleeves in three generations. The English version is clogs to clogs. The Chinese version is rice bowl to rice bowl. The Japanese, the Italians, the Spanish: practically every culture on the planet has independently arrived at some version of this observation. That independent convergence should tell us something: this is not a cultural quirk. It is a pattern so reliable, so universal, and so consistently documented that it has embedded itself into the proverb systems of civilizations that have never spoken to each other.

The financial dimension of the pattern is well-established. But this chapter is not about the money. It is about what happens to the people inside these family systems, and why the psychological dysfunction that generational wealth produces does not simply erode with the fortune. In many documented cases, it compounds. The money goes down. The crazy goes up. These are not inversely correlated by accident.

The shirtsleeves-to-shirtsleeves observation encodes a financial pattern. The psychological research adds a darker layer: the dysfunction that extreme wealth produces tends to peak in the second and third generations, precisely because the first generation still has the corrective feedback loop of having built something from nothing, while the inheriting generations have the wealth without the formative experience that produced it, and the specific parenting failures that wealth reliably generates have had more time to operate.

What the Research Actually Says About Growing Up Rich

For most of the twentieth century, developmental psychology simply did not study affluent children. The working assumption, so taken for granted it was rarely stated explicitly, was that wealthy children were fine. Better than fine. They had resources, safety, educational access, healthcare, and a thousand other advantages that researchers studying risk and resilience were busy documenting as protective factors. Why would anyone spend grant money studying children who had everything?

Suniya Luthar, then at Columbia University's Teachers College, started asking that question seriously in the 1990s and found that the answer was considerably more complicated than the assumption. Her decade-long research program on affluent youth, culminating in a widely cited 2003 paper in Child Development, 'The Culture of Affluence: Psychological Costs of Material Wealth,' and a 2005 review in Current Directions in

Psychological Science, produced findings that surprised the field and have held up through subsequent replication.

The headline finding is this: upper-class children manifest elevated rates of anxiety, depression, and substance use compared not just to middle-class peers but, in some domains, to inner-city youth from low-income families. Luthar and D'Avanzo (1999) compared suburban affluent adolescents to inner-city adolescents directly and found that the wealthy teens reported significantly higher rates of substance use. The suburban kids had more drugs, more alcohol, and more of the psychological profile associated with using both to cope.

Two mechanisms drove the pattern. The first was achievement pressure, specifically, the particular form of perfectionism that takes root when parental approval is contingent on performance rather than character. Luthar and Becker (2002) found that children whose parents overemphasized accomplishments relative to integrity showed elevated depression, anxiety, and substance use. The child learns, at a neurological level, that love is conditional on output. The appropriate coping response to that lesson, given unlimited access to pharmacological relief and no structural barriers to obtaining it, is entirely predictable.

Luthar's research identified a clinical paradox that deserves explicit attention: affluent youth are among the least likely populations to receive effective mental health intervention, despite being among the most likely to need it. The reasons are structural and they compound each other.

First, school-based mental health resources, the first-line intervention for most adolescent mental health problems, are less available to wealthy suburban students than the funding would suggest. Luthar found that school counselors in affluent districts were systematically less likely to intervene in cases of apparent distress among wealthy students, for two documented reasons: anticipated parental resistance ('that family would sue') and the assumption that wealthy children's problems were less serious or less real. The children who most needed someone to notice were in environments where the adults around them were most motivated not to notice.

Second, when affluent families do seek private therapy, which they do at higher rates than the general population, the therapeutic relationship itself is distorted by wealth dynamics. Therapists who work with wealthy families report, in clinical literature, the specific difficulty of maintaining appropriate professional challenge when the client is significantly more powerful than the therapist in every other social context, when the family's attorney is implicitly present in the room, and when the standard treatment recommendation (reduce pressure, increase connection, let the child fail in productive ways) conflicts directly with the family's fundamental operating logic. You are telling a family whose identity is organized around achievement that their child needs less achievement pressure. This is not a clinical conversation. It is a values confrontation.

Luthar's 2013 paper documented what she called 'fragility in the upper-middle classes,' a specific psychological profile in which young people from privileged backgrounds have internalized the message that their advantages obligate them to perpetual exceptional performance. 'I can, therefore I must' as an identity structure. The therapy that addresses this is not symptom management. It is identity reconstruction. It is slow, it is expensive, it often requires the parents to do their own work simultaneously, and the incentive structure of affluent family life works against every element of it at every stage.

The second mechanism was something Luthar called 'isolation from parents, both literal and emotional.' This is where the research starts to cut against a comfortable narrative. Wealthy families are assumed to be more present, more available, more engaged than families under economic stress. The data showed otherwise. Upper-middle-class secondary students were routinely left alone for significant stretches. Professional parents' careers eroded what Luthar called 'relaxed family time.' More pointedly: when Luthar compared inner-city and suburban children's perceptions of their parents across seven different dimensions of parenting quality, the suburban wealthy children scored worse on parental expectations and no differently on felt closeness to mothers and fathers, parental values emphasizing integrity, or regularity of eating dinner with parents.

This is the sentence that needs to sit for a moment: on several key dimensions of parenting quality, children from wealthy suburban families reported no significant advantage over children from low-income inner-city families. The money bought school quality, healthcare access, and neighborhood safety. It did not buy parental presence, emotional attunement, or the transmission of values over shared meals. And those latter things, it turns out, are the variables that actually protect children's psychological health.

The money bought school quality, healthcare access, and neighborhood safety. It did not buy parental presence, emotional attunement, or the transmission of values over shared meals. Those are the variables that actually protect psychological health.

The Identity Problem: Who Are You When Your Money Is Older Than You Are?

The research on affluent youth describes what happens to children growing up in wealth. But there is a distinct and somewhat more vicious problem that applies specifically to children growing up in inherited wealth: money that arrived before they did, that defines the family before the child has any opportunity to define themselves, and that immediately raises a set of identity questions that most people never have to answer.

The most fundamental of these is the question of authenticity. Tim Kasser's research program on materialism, documented most accessibly in his 2002 book The High Price of Materialism (published by MIT Press), establishes through more than a decade of empirical data that people who organize their lives around financial and material values face systematically elevated rates of anxiety, depression, low self-esteem, and difficulty with intimacy. The key word is 'organize.' Kasser is not arguing that having money causes unhappiness. He is arguing that when wealth becomes the primary lens through which a person understands their own worth and identity, when it is the answer to the question 'who am I?', it produces a specific and well-documented set of psychological costs.

Now apply this to the child born into dynastic wealth. They did not organize their life around money. Money organized itself around them, before they were born, and then got passed down. The family name carries a financial weight the child did nothing to earn and cannot easily set down. Every relationship they form comes pre-contaminated by the possibility that the other party is interested in the wealth rather than in them. Luthar's research on affluent youth documents this explicitly: wealthy children report significant difficulty trusting whether friendships are genuine or financially motivated, and this uncertainty corrodes the quality and authenticity of their social connections over time.

The inherited wealth child also faces a particular version of what psychologists call the self-concept, the internal narrative of who you are and how you came to be that way. For most people, the self-concept is built through earned experience: I did this, I survived that, I built this thing, I failed at that one and learned something useful. The narrative has causation. You feel like an agent in your own life because the evidence suggests you are. For the trust fund heir, this developmental process is profoundly disrupted. The most significant facts about their external circumstances (their housing, their education access, their healthcare, their social network, their professional opportunities) arrived as gifts rather than as outcomes of their agency. The self-concept built on that foundation is structurally unstable in ways that money cannot fix, because money is the problem rather than the solution.

This is what the colloquial 'trust fund kid' pathology is actually describing, underneath the social shorthand. Not laziness. Not stupidity. A genuine developmental impairment in the capacity to build an identity through earned consequence. The person who has never needed to push through difficulty to survive has never had the opportunity to discover that they can. The research term for the other end of this spectrum, the productive development of competence and resilience through navigating challenges, is Bandura's concept of self-efficacy: the belief, grounded in experience, that one's actions produce meaningful outcomes. Generational wealth, structurally and reliably, interferes with the formation of self-efficacy. It removes the conditions under which self-efficacy develops.

The Compounding Effect: Why the Third Generation Is the Interesting One

The first generation built the wealth. Whatever psychological distortions accompanied that building (and previous chapters have documented plenty of them), the founder at least had the experience of the building. They have a story. They know where they came from. They have a reference point for a world without the cushion, and even if that reference point has faded with time and success, it is structurally present in the identity. First-generation wealthy people often have working-class or middle-class family members who provide at least intermittent reality testing. They remember what things cost before the money. They have at minimum the memory of consequence.

The second generation grew up with money but usually within living memory of the origin story. The grandparents are still around. The founding mythology is still fresh. There is often a family business that the second generation is expected to either continue or make deliberate peace with leaving. They have inherited privilege but they have also inherited a specific gravity, a sense of obligation to the source of the wealth, a narrative about what it represents and what it cost. Second-generation pathology exists, but it is often partially counterweighted by this inherited sense of stewardship.

The third generation is where the architecture becomes genuinely precarious. By the third generation, the founder is gone. The origin story has achieved the softening quality of mythology; it is repeated at family gatherings, perhaps, but with the emotional flatness of inherited narrative rather than lived memory. The wealth has been structured into trusts, foundations, and investment vehicles. It arrives as an environment, not as a story. The third-generation heir has never experienced the world the wealth was built in, has no sensory memory of the conditions that required building it, and has no personal relationship to the person who built it. They inherit the financial outcome without any of the psychological equipment that produced it, and, critically, without any of the survival pressure that would force them to develop that equipment on their own.

Luthar's 2013 paper in Development and Psychopathology, co-authored with Barkin and Crossman, captures the result in a phrase that is both clinical and a little devastating: 'I can, therefore I must.' The fragility they document in upper-middle-class children comes not from deprivation but from the opposite, from the relentless pressure to justify, through achievement, a level of material advantage that arrived unearned. The children experience the wealth as an obligation they did nothing to incur and cannot stop being held to. The appropriate emotional response to inheriting something enormous that you did not earn and cannot return is, as it turns out, a specific flavor of anxious misery that no amount of money makes better.

Kasser's research adds a crucial layer here. He found that the insecurity driving materialistic values, the seeking of identity and worth through wealth and possessions, is not diminished by actually having wealth. It is, in many cases, amplified. The person who has always had money has never had the experience of not having it, which means they have never had the data point proving that they could survive without it. Wealth becomes not a source of security but a source of existential dependence: take it away and there is nothing beneath it that the person knows for certain they could rely on. The super-wealthy heir who clings to family money with a ferocity that baffles outside observers is not demonstrating greed in the conventional sense. They are demonstrating terror at the thought of discovering who they are without the one thing that has always defined them.

Wealth becomes not a source of security but a source of existential dependence. Take it away and there is nothing beneath it that the person knows for certain they could rely on.

What This Means for the Rest of Us, and for Democracy

This chapter has been, so far, primarily a clinical and psychological account of what happens inside wealthy families across generations. But there is a reason it belongs in a book about the relationship between extreme wealth and the social structures everyone else has to live inside. The inherited crazy is not just a private family matter. It governs institutions.

The third-generation heir who has never experienced consequence, who has never built self-efficacy through navigating difficulty, who has an identity organized almost entirely around the wealth itself, and whose psychological development was disrupted by the specific conditions Luthar and Kasser document. This person frequently ends up running things. Family-owned media companies. Agricultural holdings. Political dynasties. Endowed foundations that make funding decisions affecting research priorities, educational institutions, and charitable sectors. The particular cognitive and emotional profile produced by inherited dynastic wealth (entitlement as cognitive architecture, identity organized around the fortune, empathy deficits from an upbringing that never required navigating others' constraints, and the specific fragility that comes from never having been genuinely tested) does not disqualify a person from positions of institutional power. In many cases, the money is what positions them for it.

There is also a democratic dimension that deserves explicit naming. Every previous chapter in this book has addressed behaviors and psychological patterns that are in some sense chosen, or at minimum, behaviors to which the actor is a party. The billionaire who becomes addicted to the dopamine of accumulation has chosen to keep accumulating. The CEO who deploys moral disengagement mechanisms is making, at some level, a series of individual decisions. The philanthropist who uses charity as reputation management is exercising agency, however unconscious. The third-generation heir, by definition, did not choose any of it. They did not choose to be born into the family, did not choose the developmental environment that produced the psychological outcomes, and did not choose to inherit the power that makes their psychological profile everyone else's problem.

This is perhaps the most structurally uncomfortable finding in this chapter: the people most psychologically ill-equipped to exercise enormous institutional power are, in many cases, the people most structurally positioned to inherit it. The proverb systems of every culture on earth noted this. The developmental psychology literature documented its mechanisms. And the democratic and regulatory structures that could address it (estate taxes, inheritance limits, mandatory distribution requirements for family foundations) remain among the most politically contested policy interventions in modern governance, consistently opposed by precisely the families that the research suggests most urgently need them.

None of this is an argument against family. None of it is an argument that wealthy children deserve less love or worse parenting than anyone else. Luthar's own research concludes with explicit attention to what protective factors can counteract the documented risks: parental emotional availability, integrity-based rather than achievement-based conditional approval, and genuine relational presence. The data says what it says: these are not trivially produced in environments of extreme affluence, and producing them requires deliberate effort against structural headwinds. Families that manage it, and some do, produce children who are healthier by every psychological measure. The intervention is known. The barriers to it are documented. The costs of not doing it are being paid by everyone.

The next chapter asks what to do with all of this information, not as a spectator, but as a person who lives and works in a world these families shape. Knowing the diagnosis is one thing. Knowing how to protect yourself from it is another. That part comes next.

The most elegant feature of Stage Six is that it eventually becomes self-reproducing. The third-generation heir did not choose the psychological conditions the Cycle produced in them. Those conditions were the inheritance, more durable and more consequential than the financial assets, and considerably harder to liquidate. The Cycle doesn't just run in one lifetime. It compounds across them. Chapter Ten is where we stop analyzing the machine and start talking about how to survive it.

Chapter 11

How to Survive Them

A Practical Field Guide

You can't fix them. But you can absolutely stop letting them fix you.

Picture a Monday morning. You are walking into a meeting you did not call about a project you have been running well. You know this because the metrics are good and your team is good and three weeks ago your manager told you, in writing, that the work was on track.

The person who called the meeting begins by saying that some concerns have been raised. They don't specify by whom. They reference a conversation they had with senior leadership (again, unspecified) in which questions were surfaced about direction and execution. They express these concerns with furrowed sincerity, as though they are reluctantly delivering news that pains them. When you ask what specifically the concerns are, the answer is gestural: communication, alignment, certain stakeholders feeling uncertain. You note, carefully, that you have documented communications with all relevant stakeholders and that the last three check-ins were explicitly positive. They nod in a way that does not engage with what you just said.

By the end of the meeting, it is somehow unclear whether the problem is the project or you. You leave with an action item to 'improve visibility' and a follow-up scheduled for two weeks out. You spend the next four days trying to figure out what happened.

What happened has a name. It has been documented in peer-reviewed research. It has a three-part structure, a 30-year body of literature, and a named discoverer. And the most important thing you can know about it is this: you were not confused because the situation was confusing. You were confused because you were the target of a tactic specifically designed to produce confusion.

Nine chapters in, you know how the brain rewires around money and power. You know what hubris syndrome looks like in a boardroom and what moral disengagement looks like in a quarterly earnings call. So what do you actually do with all of this when you walk into work on Monday?

This is the chapter that answers that question. Not with platitudes. With tools drawn from the same research literature this book has been citing throughout, for recognizing what's being done to you, reducing its effectiveness, protecting yourself while you still need to be in the room, and knowing when the math has definitively changed and it is time to go.

definitively changed and it is time to go.' (end of chapter intro, before 'DARVO' section). Add new opening section 'The First Thing to Understand'.

Before the tools, one reframe. It matters more than any individual tactic in this chapter.

Most people, when they first recognize that they are dealing with someone exhibiting the patterns this book describes (the DARVO, the entitlement, the moral disengagement, the empathy deficit: they make the same initial error. They try to make the other person understand. They gather evidence. They make their case clearly and carefully. They assume that if they can just explain the impact of the behavior accurately enough, the other person will register it and respond.

This is the wrong model entirely, and understanding why it's wrong is the prerequisite for everything else in this chapter.

The research on empathy erosion from Chapter Five is directly applicable here. A person who has been through Stage Four of the Wealth Insanity Cycle, whose mirror neuron systems have been degraded by years of power insulation and who has systematically lost the feedback loops that make other people's experiences feel real, is not withholding understanding. They don't have it to give. Presenting them with clearer evidence of the impact of their behavior is like presenting someone who is colorblind with a more vivid painting. The apparatus required to process the information is not functioning. Your clarity is not the bottleneck.

This reframe is not permission to give up or to stop advocating for yourself. It is permission to stop trying to produce empathy in someone who is not currently capable of it, and to redirect that energy toward the strategies that actually work, which are, uniformly, strategies that operate through self-interest, institutional constraint, and social consequence rather than through emotional appeal.

You are not failing to communicate clearly. You are communicating clearly to someone who cannot hear it. The problem is not your message. The problem is the receiver.

The people around the powerful person can often be reached when the person themselves cannot. Institutional systems (HR, legal, compliance, regulators, boards) can be activated through documentation when direct conversation produces only DARVO. Reputational consequence, when organized collectively and documented carefully, reaches people who are impervious to individual appeals. These are the levers. The rest of this chapter is about how to use them.

Knowing the monster's weakness doesn't make you a monster. It makes you someone who survives the story.

DARVO: The Playbook You Need to Recognize Before It Runs on You

Jennifer Freyd coined the acronym DARVO in 1997 while working on betrayal trauma theory. It stands for Deny, Attack, Reverse Victim and Offender. She was describing a pattern she observed in perpetrators of abuse when confronted: they deny the conduct, attack the credibility of the person raising the concern, and then, in the move that makes it so effective, reframe the entire situation so that the person who raised the concern is now the aggressor and the person being held accountable is the victim.

For two decades, DARVO was primarily discussed in contexts of sexual misconduct and intimate partner violence. Then researchers started noticing it everywhere powerful people faced accountability: in corporate board proceedings, in political scandal responses, in institutional investigations of any kind. Because DARVO isn't a tactic specific to a particular type of harm. It is the natural behavioral output of someone with enough institutional power to make the reversal stick, a strong enough ego to perform victimhood convincingly, and sufficient resources to punish anyone who doesn't accept the new framing.

In 2017, Sarah Harsey, Eileen Zurbriggen, and Jennifer Freyd published the first empirical study directly testing DARVO as a unified concept, 'Perpetrator Responses to Victim Confrontation: DARVO and Victim Self-Blame,' in the Journal of Aggression, Maltreatment, and Trauma. The findings were not encouraging for anyone who has faced DARVO and tried to push through it: DARVO was commonly used by people who were confronted; higher exposure to DARVO during a confrontation was associated with greater victim self-blame; and the three components of the pattern correlated with each other, confirming it as a unified strategy rather than three separate coincidental behaviors.

Harsey and Freyd's subsequent experimental work (2020) tightened this further. Participants exposed to a DARVO response in a vignette rated the perpetrator as less abusive and less responsible, and the victim as less believable and more to blame, compared to participants who received a neutral response to the same underlying facts. DARVO doesn't have to persuade people of the perpetrator's innocence. It only has to muddy the waters sufficiently that the truth seems complicated, contested, and not worth the social cost of siding with the person raising it.

The good news from the same research program: education about DARVO reduces its effectiveness. In Harsey and Freyd's experimental design, participants who were briefed on how DARVO works before encountering it in a vignette were significantly less likely to blame the victim and more likely to accurately assess the perpetrator's responsibility. The inoculation effect is real. Knowing the name of what's being done to you is a countermeasure, not just a comfort.

DARVO doesn't need to prove innocence. It only needs to make the truth seem complicated, contested, and not worth the social cost of siding with the person raising it.

So: what does DARVO look like in a professional context with a wealthy, powerful person? The template is consistent enough to be recognizable once you know what you're watching for.

Deny looks like: categorical rejection of the specific incident, combined with a broader assertion of general virtue ('I have always treated my employees fairly,' 'No one has ever raised this concern before,' 'I have an open-door policy'). The denial is rarely confined to the specific facts. It expands to character: theirs, impeccable; yours, suddenly suspect.

Attack looks like: questioning your competence, your motives, your mental state, your employment history, your performance record, and sometimes your relationships with other people in the organization. The attack need not be loud to be effective. A well-timed 'I've been getting some concerning feedback about [your name]' to someone you need as an ally is an attack. So is a performance review that materializes six weeks after you raised a concern.

Reverse Victim and Offender looks like: the conversation shifting from what they did to how your raising of it has damaged them. The stress it has caused. The sleepless nights. The reputational harm to someone who has 'given so much' to this organization. The implication that you owe them something (gratitude, loyalty, silence) and that your refusal to provide it is the actual injury in the room.

Once you can see the three-beat structure in real time, something changes. The self-blame that DARVO is designed to produce (the wondering whether you're overreacting, whether you misremembered, whether you're causing more harm than you're preventing) loses some of its grip. You are not confused because the situation is confusing. You are confused because a documented manipulation tactic is specifically designed to produce confusion. Those are different problems with different solutions.

The Gray Rock Method: Surviving When You Can't Yet Leave

Cutting contact with a powerful, manipulative person is the cleanest solution. It is also frequently unavailable, at least immediately. The wealthy founder whose company you work for is also the person whose signature is on your paycheck. The controlling family member with inherited money is also the person whose name is on the trust that funds your children's education. The well-connected senior partner is also the person who controls referrals in your industry. Sometimes the correct long-term answer is obvious and the short-term problem is survival while you build the exit.

The gray rock method is a behavioral strategy that emerged from abuse survivor communities, primarily through a 2012 blog post by a writer named Skylar who was processing her own escape from a manipulative relationship. It was not developed in a research laboratory, and the scientific literature on its effectiveness is limited; there are no randomized controlled trials of gray rocking. What there are is a substantial body of convergent clinical observations, a clear behavioral logic grounded in operant conditioning principles, and enough anecdotal documentation across diverse contexts to take seriously.

The principle is simple. Manipulative people (and the research on narcissism, hubris syndrome, and entitlement from earlier chapters documents why high-power wealthy individuals so frequently fall into this category) require an emotional reaction from others. The reaction is not incidental to the manipulation; it is the goal. Control, status assertion, and the particular pleasure of dominating someone's emotional state all require the target to have emotional states that can be dominated. If you provide no emotional reaction worth having, you become, from the manipulator's perspective, uninteresting. A gray rock. Something they step over on the way to someone more responsive.

In practice, gray rocking in a professional context means: responding to provocations with flat, brief, transactional language. No defensiveness. No visible distress. No visible anger. No elaborate explanations that the other person can mine for vulnerabilities. 'I'll look into that.' 'Thanks for letting me know.' 'That's noted.' Keep your tone the color of conference room carpet. Give them nothing that rewards the behavior with the reaction it was designed to produce.

The risks are real and deserve honest naming. Some individuals escalate when their usual manipulation tactics fail to produce results; the initial response to gray rocking can be intensification rather than withdrawal, and if the person has enough institutional power, escalation is dangerous. Gray rocking also carries a psychological cost for the person doing it: suppressing genuine emotional responses is exhausting, and it is not a sustainable long-term strategy in any context where you have significant ongoing contact with the person. Clinical psychologists who discuss the method are consistent on this point: it is a bridge tool, not a permanent state. The bridge leads somewhere specific: documentation, ally-building, and exit planning.

Documentation is the part of this chapter that people resist most, because it requires them to accept a reality they'd rather not accept: that they are, or may soon be, in an adversarial relationship with someone who has more institutional power than they do. Starting a documentation habit feels like a declaration of war. It is not. It is an insurance policy.

The specific documentation practices that matter most are: contemporaneous records (written notes made at the time of the incident, not reconstructed later; courts and HR processes weight contemporaneous records significantly more than recalled accounts); date-stamped communications (email confirmations of verbal conversations, 'just following up in writing on what we discussed,' which creates a paper record even when the other party declines to confirm anything); and a timeline document that organizes incidents chronologically with specific dates, witnesses where present, and impact on your work performance.

The timeline document serves two functions. Practically, it is the foundation of any HR complaint, legal consultation, or regulatory report. Psychologically, it is a counter to the gaslighting that typically accompanies sustained DARVO: when you have written records of what was said, when, and by whom, the 'you're misremembering' and 'that never happened' moves lose traction. Your own records are an anchor to reality when the environment is designed to make reality feel unstable.

One specific note on HR, because the research on organizational dynamics is clear about this: HR departments work for the organization, not for you. This is not a cynical observation; it is their legal and professional mandate. They are trained to protect the institution from liability, which sometimes aligns with protecting you and sometimes does not. Before filing a formal HR complaint, it is worth consulting an employment attorney (many offer initial consultations at low or no cost) to understand what protections apply in your specific jurisdiction, what filing triggers and what it forecloses, and whether the organizational culture has a track record of institutional DARVO (filing complaints that then 'mysteriously' result in the complainant's performance being scrutinized) or genuine investigation.

Gray rocking is not surrender. It is refusing to give the reaction that powers the game. The goal is not to be unaffected. It is to appear unaffected long enough to get your pieces into position.

The Documentation Imperative: What You Write Down, You Can Use

There is a sequence that plays out with some regularity in professional disputes involving powerful, wealthy individuals, and it goes roughly like this: something happens. You raise a concern. DARVO unfolds. Suddenly there is a contested account of whether the original thing happened at all, and the only evidence is your word against someone with ten times your institutional capital. The contested account is not primarily resolved by truth. It is resolved by documentation, witnesses, and the asymmetric ability of each party to sustain the social cost of the dispute.

You can't change the asymmetry in institutional capital. You can change the documentation situation.

Write things down contemporaneously. The legal standard for the credibility of contemporaneous records, notes made at or near the time of an event before any dispute has materialized, is significantly higher than the credibility of recollections reconstructed after the fact. An email you sent to yourself at 6:47 PM on a Tuesday describing exactly what was said in a meeting that afternoon is substantially more defensible than your memory of the same meeting recalled eighteen months later during a deposition. The date stamp matters. The detail matters. The absence of any obvious retrospective motivation matters.

What to document: specific statements, with direct quotes where possible. The names of everyone present. Any witnesses to the particular exchange. Any follow-up communications (emails, texts, messages) that reference or confirm the substance of what happened. Any changes in your working conditions, assignments, performance reviews, or social standing that occur in proximity to raising a concern. The timeline is your friend. A performance improvement plan that materializes six weeks after a complaint is a fact. Its timing adjacent to that complaint is also a fact. Both facts in sequence tell a story that neither fact tells alone.

Send contemporaneous emails to yourself from work accounts when appropriate, or to personal accounts if you have reason to believe the work account may not be safe. Some jurisdictions have specific rules about whether you can document workplace conversations; know what applies in yours. If your workplace has an Employee Relations, HR, or Ethics function, understand its actual reporting architecture, specifically whether the function reports to the CEO, to the board, to Legal, or to an independent oversight body. HR reporting to the person you're raising a concern about is a structural conflict that does not resolve in your favor. Knowing this before you file a complaint is significantly more useful than knowing it after.

Build your witness network before you need it. Not as a mobilization toward confrontation (that's usually counterproductive), but simply as a practice of maintaining professional relationships outside the orbit of the person you're concerned about. Isolation is one of the most reliable precursors to successful manipulation. People who are professionally isolated have no corroborating witnesses, no one to notice when their situation changes, and no one whose perspective hasn't been shaped by the person controlling the environment. The antidote is not paranoia. It is broad professional relationships maintained with normal human decency.

The Exit Calculus: When to Escalate, When to Endure, When to Leave

Everything above assumes you are trying to survive within a system while you figure out your options. That is a reasonable place to be. It is not a permanent place to be. At some point the calculation changes, and the chapter would be irresponsible if it didn't name the signals.

The first signal that endurance has become untenable is when the cost of staying exceeds the cost of leaving in a way that has become measurable in your health, relationships, or sense of self. This sounds obvious stated directly. In practice, people in high-control relationships with powerful individuals, professional or personal, are often the last to recognize how fully the cost has accumulated, because the manipulation that makes leaving difficult is the same manipulation that makes the cost of staying hard to see clearly. The research on trauma bonding, organizational culture, and manufactured dependency all document the cognitive mechanisms by which people's threshold for 'too much' shifts over time in environments of sustained pressure and intermittent reward.

An external reference point helps. What would you tell a friend in your situation? That question produces answers that the internal normalization process suppresses. If the answer is 'leave' or 'get out' or 'that is not okay,' start listening to it.

The second signal is when the organization itself has become the instrument of the harm, when HR is running interference rather than investigating, when the legal team's job is your exposure rather than your protection, when the internal escalation paths have been systematically closed or controlled. Freyd's concept of institutional DARVO, when institutions collectively execute the deny-attack-reverse pattern to protect powerful actors and silence those raising concerns, describes exactly this configuration. An institution committed to institutional DARVO cannot be reformed from inside by individuals with less institutional power than the people whose behavior they're contesting. The appropriate response is external: regulatory bodies, legal counsel independent of the organization, industry oversight where it exists, and, where appropriate and legally defensible, public accountability.

The third signal is a physical one: when your body is giving you the fight-or-flight data that your rational mind is finding reasons to override. Chronic sleep disruption, persistent anxiety that doesn't resolve between interactions, physical symptoms that appear reliably before or after contact with the person in question. The body is not being dramatic. It is processing information that the cognitive override is suppressing. Give it some credibility.

The exit calculus is not always about dramatic confrontation and legal action. Sometimes it is simply about having, before you need it, the financial runway and professional network that makes leaving possible. Build those things now, in the good times, before you're making decisions in a crisis. The person who has three months of savings, active relationships outside their current organization, and a resume that doesn't depend entirely on references from the person they're concerned about has options that the person without those things doesn't. Options are dignity. Dignity is worth building toward while there's still time to build.

One final observation, because this book has been about systems and not just individuals: the tactics in this chapter are necessary and valuable, and they are also insufficient at scale. The patterns described in the previous nine chapters are not produced by individual bad actors who can be gray-rocked into irrelevance. They are produced by systems that reward specific cognitive profiles, protect the people those profiles inhabit, and externalize the costs onto everyone else. Individual survival strategy is how you get through the week. Systemic change is how the week becomes different for the people who come after you. The next chapter is about that.

The Wealth Insanity Cycle operates at the institutional level, but its effects are felt at the interpersonal one, in meetings, in performance reviews, in the specific Monday mornings that prompted you to pick up this book. The tools in this chapter are about interrupting the Cycle where it touches your actual life. Chapter Eleven is about interrupting it at the level where the pipe actually runs.

Chapter 12

The Deference Disease

Why We Protect the People Hurting Us, and How to Stop

In 1972, psychologist Philip Zimbardo ran what became the most famous and most frequently misrepresented experiment in the history of social science. Twenty-four psychologically healthy college students were randomly assigned to play either guards or prisoners in a simulated jail in the basement of Stanford's psychology building. The experiment was scheduled to run two weeks. Zimbardo stopped it after six days because the 'guards' had become genuinely sadistic and the 'prisoners' had begun exhibiting signs of genuine psychological breakdown.

The Stanford Prison Experiment has been criticized on methodological grounds, some substantially valid, and its replication record is complicated. But the underlying phenomenon Zimbardo was trying to study, the human capacity to defer to authority, to internalize assigned roles, and to accept arrangements that are visibly harmful, is among the most robustly documented findings in all of social psychology. Stanley Milgram had already established it in 1963. Solomon Asch had established the conformity version of it in the 1950s. The SPE added an ugly specific: people don't just obey authority when commanded. They actively perform it. They become it.

This chapter is about the collective version of that phenomenon. Not the individual trapped in a coercive relationship (Chapter Ten covered the toolkit for that), but the broader social and psychological dynamics that cause populations to protect, celebrate, and defer to the wealthy and powerful people who are, by the evidence of the preceding ten chapters, disproportionately likely to be harming them.

This is the part of the book that is the most uncomfortable. Not because the research is surprising (it isn't), but because it implicates all of us. Not in the sense of moral failing. In the sense of cognitive architecture.

The Obedience Infrastructure

Milgram's obedience research is usually summarized as: ordinary people will do terrible things when an authority figure tells them to. This is accurate but incomplete. The more precise finding, the one that matters for understanding collective deference to wealth and power, is about what conditions produced obedience and what conditions reduced it.

In the baseline condition of Milgram's shock experiments, approximately 65 percent of participants administered what they believed were potentially lethal electric shocks to another person when instructed to by an authority figure in a lab coat. When the authority figure was absent, giving instructions by phone rather than in person, compliance dropped to 20 percent. When the participant could see the victim, being in the same room rather than separated by a wall, compliance dropped further. When other participants (who were confederates) refused to continue, compliance dropped to 10 percent.

The variables that reduced obedience were: physical distance from authority, physical proximity to the victim, and the presence of dissenting peers. The variables that increased it were: the apparent legitimacy and status of the authority, the incremental escalation of the request (no one was asked to start at maximum shock), and the absence of social permission to deviate from the commanded behavior.

Map this onto the conditions that wealthy and powerful people have systematically constructed around themselves and the pattern becomes legible. Executive suites are physically and socially distant from the people affected by the decisions made in them. The human consequences of corporate decisions are abstracted, represented in spreadsheets, reports, and euphemistic language rather than present as embodied human beings in the same room. Dissent is structurally penalized; the corporate cultures documented in Chapter Three actively select against people who challenge authority, and the economic insecurity that characterizes most working people's lives makes the cost of public dissent genuinely high. And the legitimacy scaffolding around extreme wealth (the meritocracy narrative, the philanthropic branding, the media architecture of deference) described in the previous chapter, functions as the lab coat. It signals: this authority is legitimate. Compliance is appropriate.

Milgram's lab coat didn't make the authority real. It made it feel real. The meritocracy narrative is a very large, very expensive lab coat worn by an entire economic class.

This is not a metaphor designed to be uncharitable. It is a structural comparison that has direct empirical support. The conditions that produce obedience in Milgram's paradigm map with uncomfortable precision to the conditions that characterize working people's relationship to concentrated economic power.

Awe, Status, and the Halo Effect

There is a second mechanism operating alongside obedience: the halo effect, and its specific amplification in the presence of wealth and status.

The halo effect, the tendency to attribute positive qualities to people who are appealing in one domain on the basis of that appeal alone, is one of the most replicated findings in social psychology. First documented by psychologist Edward Thorndike in 1920, it has been confirmed across hundreds of studies in employment, education, criminal justice, and politics. Attractive people are perceived as more intelligent, more competent, more honest. Tall people are perceived as better leaders. Directly relevant here: wealthy people are perceived as more capable, more meritorious, and more worthy of deference, by virtue of their wealth alone.

A 2017 study by psychologists Joey Cheng, Jessica Tracy, and Joseph Henrich published in Evolution and Human Behavior documented two distinct pathways to high social status in human groups: dominance (achieved through intimidation, coercion, and the threat of harm) and prestige (achieved through demonstrated skill, knowledge, or success that others want to learn from). The two pathways produce different follower behaviors: dominance produces fear-based deference, prestige produces genuine admiration; but both produce deference. And critically, people are not reliable at distinguishing between them. The behavioral signals of dominance and prestige overlap sufficiently that observers frequently misattribute one for the other, particularly when they lack direct knowledge of how the status was achieved.

In the context of extreme wealth, this matters enormously. Extreme wealth signals success. Success signals prestige. Prestige produces genuine admiration, deference, and the cognitive extensions of the halo effect, the assumption of competence in domains beyond the one where the success was demonstrated. The tech founder who made a successful consumer app is perceived as having insight into economic policy, geopolitics, and human nature that has nothing to do with their demonstrated domain of competence. The investor who correctly identified profitable opportunities in a particular market is assumed to have wisdom about social arrangements, human motivation, and the proper structure of institutions that his track record does not actually support.

We give wealthy people credit for things they haven't demonstrated, and we do it automatically, not as a deliberate judgment, but as a cognitive extension of a status signal that our social primate brains are not well-equipped to evaluate critically.

for things they haven't demonstrated, and we do it automatically.' called 'The Celebrity Billionaire as Cultural Technology'.

The halo effect and status-prestige confusion have existed for as long as humans have organized themselves into hierarchies. What is genuinely new in the last thirty years is the specific cultural technology that amplifies and accelerates both: the celebrity billionaire.

The celebrity billionaire is a specific media construct, a wealthy person transformed through deliberate media strategy and cultural absorption, into a figure of popular fascination whose private life, opinions, and daily activities are followed with the intensity previously reserved for entertainment performers. The construct is new. Howard Hughes had elements of it. The Rockefellers had their tabloid moments. But the systematic production of wealthy people as celebrities, with PR teams, social media presences, profiles in general-interest publications, podcast appearances, documentary subjects, and fan communities organized around their personalities, is a post-2000 phenomenon, and it is doing specific and underexamined work in the political economy of wealth.

The celebrity billionaire functions as a delivery system for the halo effect at population scale. When millions of people follow the daily activities of a wealthy person (his opinions on geopolitics, her workout routine, their philosophical musings on human nature), they are receiving a continuous, low-grade signal that this person's thoughts and judgments deserve attention across domains unrelated to the specific domain in which they achieved success. The parasocial relationship, the one-sided intimacy that media creates between audience and subject, is structurally identical to the cognitive mechanism that makes us defer to prestige: we feel like we know them, we feel like they've earned our trust, we feel like their confidence in their own judgment is warranted because we've been immersed in their world.

Researcher Crystal Abidin, who studies influencer culture, has documented how parasocial relationships specifically reduce critical scrutiny of the subject's claims and positions. The audience member who feels they 'know' a celebrity billionaire processes that person's statements about policy, economics, or social organization through a different cognitive filter than they would apply to a stranger making the same claims. The familiarity override is real, it is measurable, and it is being deliberately cultivated by communications teams whose job is to produce exactly this effect.

The political consequence is direct. Celebrity billionaires who have large and devoted followings can shift public opinion on policy questions, not by making superior arguments, but by making familiar ones. The trust transfer from personal appeal to policy position is a documented feature of parasocial relationships in general and has been measured specifically in the context of wealthy influential figures. When someone you feel you know and trust expresses contempt for a particular policy proposal, the contempt lands differently than it would from a stranger. The halo does the persuasion. The argument is almost incidental.

The celebrity billionaire is not a person who became famous. It is a media format designed to make a person feel like someone you trust, and then to use that trust for purposes the audience did not consent to.

Identification With the Aggressor, at Scale

There is a third mechanism, the most uncomfortable of the three, that requires being addressed directly: the psychological phenomenon that Anna Freud called 'identification with the aggressor' and that modern trauma researchers have extended into the broader concept of traumatic bonding.

In its clinical form, identification with the aggressor describes the tendency of people in coercive or abusive relationships to adopt the perspective, values, and even the defense of the person exercising power over them. The prisoner who internalizes the prison's logic. The child who explains why their abusive parent was right. The hostage who comes to feel genuine affection for their captor (a phenomenon so consistent it has its own name, 'Stockholm syndrome,' coined after a 1973 Swedish bank robbery in which hostages defended their captors to police after their release.

The clinical literature on this phenomenon is extensive. The mechanisms are well-documented: when a person is in a position of dependency and vulnerability relative to a more powerful actor, identifying with that actor's perspective is an adaptive survival strategy. If I can predict what you want, present myself as aligned with your interests, and avoid triggering your aggression by never positioning myself as your adversary, I am safer than I would be if I maintained an adversarial stance. The identification is not chosen. It is a functional response to an environment of constrained options.

The question this chapter is asking is whether something analogous, not identical, not as severe, but structurally similar, operates at the collective level in relation to economic power. And the evidence suggests: yes. With important caveats about scale and mechanism, but yes.

Political psychologist Jim Sidanius and his colleagues developed Social Dominance Theory, the framework that has generated the most robust empirical research on this question, over several decades beginning in the 1990s. The theory proposes that all human social systems generate hierarchies, that those hierarchies produce group-based inequality, and that a specific psychological orientation, 'social dominance orientation' (SDO), predicts the degree to which individuals support and maintain those hierarchies. High-SDO individuals prefer group-based inequality and support the institutional arrangements that sustain it. Low-SDO individuals prefer equality and challenge those arrangements.

What makes SDO research directly relevant here is its consistent finding about who holds high versus low SDO orientations, and specifically, the finding that subordinated group members frequently show elevated SDO: supporting the hierarchy that disadvantages them. This is the empirical analog of identification with the aggressor at the population level. Not Stockholm syndrome exactly, but a measurable pattern in which people who are disadvantaged by a hierarchical arrangement nonetheless support its legitimacy and stability.

The most elegant feature of a well-functioning hierarchy is that it eventually doesn't need guards. The people at the bottom become invested in their own containment.

Sidanius and Pratto, in their 1999 book Social Dominance: An Intergroup Theory of Social Hierarchy and Oppression, documented this pattern across multiple societies, multiple hierarchical dimensions (race, class, gender), and multiple measurement instruments. The findings are robust and uncomfortable: subordinated people support their own subordination at rates that cannot be explained by misinformation alone. The psychological machinery of deference is doing something more fundamental than simply keeping people from accessing the truth.

What Breaks the Spell

This chapter has established three mechanisms that sustain collective deference to concentrated wealth and power: the obedience infrastructure (authority, legitimacy, incremental escalation, absence of visible dissent), the halo effect and status-prestige confusion, and the identification-with-the-aggressor dynamic operating at population scale through SDO.

These are not insurmountable. They have been interrupted before. Understanding what interrupts them is the practical utility of naming them.

The Milgram research identified the most powerful interruption clearly: the presence of dissenting peers. When other participants refused to continue, compliance dropped from 65 percent to 10 percent. This is not a small effect. It is the difference between most people complying and almost no one complying, produced by a single variable: visible social permission to deviate. The spell broke not because people suddenly had new information, but because someone else had already broken it. The first person to say the emperor has no clothes is doing something genuinely difficult. The second person is doing something much easier. The third person barely has to do anything at all.

The halo effect is interrupted by specific competence information, evidence that the status signal in one domain does not transfer to another. Research on the halo effect consistently finds that it is weakened by concrete negative information in the non-halo domain. When people are given specific, credible evidence that a high-status person is incompetent in the domain they're being deferred to, the deference reduces. This is why the case study work in this book matters: not just as illustration, but as evidence that the halo, the assumption of general competence from domain-specific success, is falsified by the record.

Social Dominance Orientation is reduced by exposure to what researchers call 'hierarchy-attenuating' institutional environments: contexts in which equal-status contact is structurally enforced, where cross-group collaboration is required, and where status hierarchies are explicitly de-emphasized. The research finding most directly relevant here is that SDO is not stable across contexts; it responds to environmental signals about the legitimacy and permeability of hierarchies. People who are shown credible evidence that hierarchies are constructed rather than natural, permeable rather than fixed, and costly rather than inevitable tend to show reduced SDO. The Myth Machine described in the previous chapter works by providing the opposite signals. Interrupting it requires providing these ones instead.

None of this is fast. None of it is simple. But the mechanisms are known, which means the points of intervention are known too. The deference is not hardwired. It is maintained by conditions. Change the conditions and the deference changes with them.

hardwired. It is maintained by conditions. Change the conditions and the deference changes with them.' (end of 'What Breaks the Spell'

The three mechanisms described in this chapter (obedience infrastructure, halo effect/status confusion, and identification with the aggressor at population scale) can feel paralyzing when named this explicitly. The scale is large. The mechanisms are deep. The cultural reinforcement is continuous. This is a reasonable thing to feel.

The research offers two specific and empirically grounded responses to that feeling.

The first is that these mechanisms are, as noted above, context-dependent. They respond to environmental signals. The specific environmental signals that reduce them are: peer visibility of dissent, concrete counterevidence in the non-halo domain, and exposure to information about how the hierarchy was built rather than treating it as natural. All three of these are things that individuals can, in ordinary life, contribute to, by speaking about their own economic experience honestly rather than performing a prosperity that doesn't exist, by naming specifically when a wealthy person's domain expertise is being extended beyond its demonstrated range, and by knowing and sharing the policy history that produced current arrangements rather than treating the current arrangement as the baseline.

The second is that the scale of change doesn't have to be political to matter. Solomon Asch's conformity experiments found that the presence of a single ally, one other person who named what they were seeing accurately, reduced conformity dramatically. Not eliminated it. Reduced it. The person who says, in a meeting, 'I notice that we're deferring to this view because of who's expressing it rather than because of the evidence for it' is doing something small that is also, in aggregate, significant. The dissenting peer who broke the spell in Milgram's experiments was not trying to change the world. They were just refusing to keep going. That is enough to make a difference. It has been demonstrated experimentally. It can be done by anyone.

Chapter Eleven is about the larger-scale version of those same acts.

Chapter 13

Fix the System, Not the Symptoms

What Structural Change Actually Looks Like

Individual crazy is a personal problem. Systemic crazy is a policy problem. The difference is who gets to decide it's someone else's fault.

In 1911, the Triangle Shirtwaist Factory in New York City caught fire. One hundred and forty-six workers died, most of them young immigrant women. They died because the factory owners had locked the exit doors to prevent unauthorized breaks. They died because there were no sprinklers. They died because the fire escapes collapsed under the weight of people trying to use them. They died because no regulation required anything different.

The owners, Max Blanck and Isaac Harris, were acquitted of manslaughter charges. They collected the insurance payout. They paid $75 per deceased victim in civil settlements, approximately $2,300 in today's dollars, and returned to the garment business.

What happened next is the part that matters for this chapter. The fire did not produce charity. It produced legislation. The New York State Factory Investigating Commission conducted 3,385 inspections and filed 56 new pieces of legislation covering fire safety, sanitation, working hours, and child labor. Frances Perkins, who would later become the first female cabinet secretary as

Franklin Roosevelt's Secretary of Labor, watched women jump from the burning building and spent the following decades turning that experience into structural policy. The New Deal's labor protections were built, in meaningful part, on the foundation of what the Triangle fire made politically possible.

The response to the Triangle fire was not grief, followed by a support group for survivors, followed by a self-help book on how to gray-rock a dangerous employer. It was grief, followed by organized political action, followed by laws that changed the physical conditions in which workers operated. The pipe was identified. The pipe was fixed. The deaths stopped.

Here is a thought experiment to start the final chapter.

Imagine a factory that has been, for decades, quietly pumping a specific toxin into the local water supply. The toxin produces a predictable syndrome in people who drink it long enough: elevated aggression, reduced empathy, impaired social judgment, and an inflated belief in their own importance relative to everyone around them. Some people drink more of it than others. The more they drink, the worse the syndrome. The syndrome is well-documented. Researchers have published extensively on it. You have now read eleven chapters about it.

Now imagine that the community response to the toxin is: individual therapy for the people who've been drinking it, support groups for people who've been harmed by them, and self-help books for everyone else on how to recognize the syndrome and gray-rock their way through interactions with affected individuals.

This is useful. It is genuinely useful. People need coping strategies while they're still downstream from the pipe. Chapter Ten was that. But at some point, someone has to look upstream, find the pipe, and turn it off. The therapy and support groups and self-help books don't do that. They manage the consequences of the pipe. The pipe keeps running.

This book has spent ten chapters mapping the syndrome: the neuroscience of how money rewires the brain, the psychology of how power erodes empathy, the sociology of how entitlement reproduces itself across generations, the institutional dynamics of how the same patterns capture organizations and policy in predictable ways. The syndrome is real, it's well-documented, and it is produced by a system that was built by people operating under particular incentives at particular historical moments.

That last part matters more than it usually gets credit for. Systems built by people can be rebuilt by people. Not easily. Not quickly. Not without significant organized resistance from the people who benefit most from the current configuration. But the current arrangement is not a law of physics. It is a set of policy choices that can be made differently.

You don't fix a flooding basement by bailing water faster. You fix the pipe. Time to find the pipe.

What the Historical Record Actually Shows

Before getting to the policy toolkit, it's worth being honest about the historical evidence, including the parts of it that get used as bumper stickers in ways that overstate what actually happened.

The United States between approximately 1933 and the mid-1970s is frequently cited as proof that extreme wealth concentration can be significantly reduced without economic collapse. The citation is correct. The mechanism is somewhat more complicated than the shorthand version.

The New Deal era established institutional structures (labor protections, banking regulations, public investment programs, social insurance systems) that changed the structural conditions under which wealth accumulated and was distributed. The Revenue Acts of 1935, 1937, and 1942 pushed the top marginal income tax rate from 25 percent in 1932 to 94 percent by 1944, where it remained above 90 percent continuously through 1963, spanning the Truman, Eisenhower, and Kennedy administrations across two parties. The 91 percent rate applied only to income above $200,000, equivalent to roughly $2 to $3 million in today's dollars, and affected fewer than 10,000 households in the entire country. This was not a broad tax on professional success. It was a structural ceiling on dynastic accumulation by a tiny fraction of the population.

Here is the complication that the historical-precedent argument requires: the nominal rate and the effective rate were very different things. Research by Piketty and Saez documents that the top 1 percent during the 1950s paid an average effective income tax rate of roughly 16.9 percent, not 91 percent, because the high nominal rates existed alongside an extensive system of shelters, deductions, and accounting arrangements that reduced taxable income substantially. The 91 percent bracket was a ceiling that shaped behavior, constrained ostentatious accumulation, and funded significant public investment, but it was not a simple rate that nine of every ten dollars above the threshold were handed over. The Tax Foundation analysis of this period is worth engaging with honestly: the rich were not paying dramatically more than today, measured in effective rates, though the absolute revenue collected was higher and the structural inequality far lower.

What this means for the current debate: the honest argument for restoring substantially higher top marginal rates is not 'it worked perfectly before.' It's that the combination of high nominal rates, constrained sheltering options, strong labor institutions, and robust public investment produced a significantly less unequal society, and that the Reagan-era dismantling of that combination, which cut the top rate from 70 percent to 28 percent between 1981 and 1988 while simultaneously weakening labor protections, produced measurably higher inequality over the following four decades. The causation argument is supported by the timing and the cross-country comparisons, even if the mechanism is not simply 'higher rates = more revenue.'

The system that produces wealth pathology was not inevitable. It was built through specific policy choices made at specific historical moments. That means it can be rebuilt through different choices. The only question is whether enough people decide that it should be.

The Nordic comparison is more instructive than the American historical one, because it is current and observable rather than contested memory. A 2023 NBER working paper on income equality in the Nordic countries (Denmark, Norway, Sweden, Finland) finds that Nordic income equality is primarily driven by a significant compression of hourly wages achieved through coordinated wage bargaining systems with strong union involvement, rather than primarily through redistribution via the tax-transfer system alone. This is important: the Nordic model is not simply 'tax the rich and give it to the poor.' It is a system in which the pre-distribution structure (who gets what before taxes are calculated) is itself shaped by institutional rules that give workers meaningful bargaining power.

Denmark provides a particularly clean natural experiment on wealth taxation. Research by Jakobsen, Jakobsen, Kleven, and Zucman, published in the Quarterly Journal of Economics in 2020, uses the 1989 Danish wealth tax reform as a quasi-experiment to estimate behavioral responses to wealth taxation. Their core finding: wealth inequality in Denmark stabilized significantly relative to the United States from the late 1990s onward, with Denmark's top 1 percent holding roughly 20 percent of total wealth by 2012 compared to nearly 40 percent in the United States. The policy architecture is different. The outcomes are measurably different. The gap between Denmark's and America's wealth distribution widened specifically during the period when American policy moved in the opposite direction from Denmark's.

None of this is an argument that any particular policy proposal is costless or that the Nordic model translates without friction to a country with different institutional history, political culture, and economic structure. It is an argument that the outcome of current American inequality is not inevitable, is not the natural result of neutral market forces, and has international and historical precedents for looking substantially different.

The Policy Toolkit: What the Evidence Supports

The research literature on wealth concentration and inequality reduction points toward a coherent set of policy interventions. None of them are original. Most have been debated seriously for decades. The reason they haven't been implemented is not that economists haven't figured out what works. It's that the people who would pay for them have enough institutional power to prevent implementation. Naming that plainly is itself a form of analytical honesty that the policy debate often lacks.

Progressive wealth taxation is the most direct structural intervention. Thomas Piketty's Capital in the Twenty-First Century (2014) made the theoretical case for an annual progressive wealth tax, not just income taxation but a levy on accumulated wealth itself, as a mechanism to interrupt the compounding dynamic by which wealth begets more wealth faster than economies grow. The Piketty-Saez-Zucman research program has since developed the empirical architecture supporting this argument. Emmanuel Saez and Gabriel Zucman's 2019 work simulating the impact of a progressive wealth tax on Forbes 400 wealth concentration since 1982 demonstrates that even modest annual rates (in the range of 2 to 8 percent on wealth above threshold levels) can meaningfully reduce top-end concentration over time through what they call the 'mechanical effect': the mathematical reality that taxing wealth annually at rates exceeding returns on lower-risk assets prevents compounding from operating unboundedly.

The design challenges are real and documented. European wealth taxes implemented during the twentieth century in Germany, Switzerland, Sweden, France, and Spain suffered from four main structural weaknesses, as Saez and Zucman describe: they applied only to some asset classes and not others, creating avoidance incentives; they lacked adequate information reporting; they had insufficient enforcement; and they operated without international coordination, making wealth flight a genuine behavioral response. Sweden's top wealth tax rate reached 4 percent in the early 1980s, applied in addition to income and inheritance taxes, and was eventually abolished in 2007 partly due to capital flight concerns. These are design problems, not proof that the concept fails. A well-designed wealth tax with comprehensive asset coverage, third-party reporting requirements, and international information-sharing agreements addresses the avoidance mechanisms that undermined the European precedents.

Inheritance and estate taxation addresses the intergenerational transmission documented extensively in Chapter Nine. The United States currently has an estate tax that applies only to estates above $13.6 million per individual (as of 2024), with a top rate of 40 percent and a documented avoidance industry of lawyers, financial planners, and trust structures that reduce effective rates well below the nominal ceiling. Research by Piketty and Saez on optimal inheritance tax formulas establishes that the key parameters are behavioral elasticities, how much heirs reduce their own accumulation in response to inheritance taxes, distributional parameters, and social preferences for how much intergenerational wealth transfer a society wants to permit. The optimal formula is not infinite taxation that confiscates all inherited wealth; it is a progressive structure that meaningfully reduces the transmission of extreme dynastic advantage while allowing normal intergenerational support. What the current U.S. system does not do: meaningfully interrupt the third-generation pathology documented in Chapter Nine.

Corporate governance reform is less discussed in the inequality literature than taxation but arguably as important for addressing wealth pathology at the source rather than the symptom. The research in Chapters Three and Four on corporate psychopathy and the power-disinhibition dynamic documents how the fiduciary structure of publicly traded corporations (maximize shareholder value, minimize all other considerations) creates institutional selection pressure for precisely the cognitive profiles associated with wealth pathology. A legal architecture that requires directors to consider employee welfare, community impact, and long-term sustainability in addition to shareholder returns changes the selection pressure at the top of major institutions. Germany's codetermination system, which requires worker representation on corporate supervisory boards, is one documented model. The evidence on its effects on wage distribution, labor relations, and corporate risk-taking over several decades provides a comparison point that the American corporate governance debate largely ignores.

Campaign finance and political influence disclosure is the intervention that precedes all others, because the current concentration of political influence in the hands of large donors is the structural mechanism by which the other interventions get blocked. The research cited in Chapter Eight on donor-advised funds noted that 100 billionaire families spent approximately $2.6 billion influencing elections in a recent cycle, a figure that represents a small fraction of their wealth and a significant fraction of the money shaping what policy options are considered viable. Addressing the money-in-politics problem is not separate from the wealth-concentration problem. It is the same problem operating in a different domain.

What You Can Actually Do: A Graded Action List

This is the part of the final chapter where books sometimes hand you a list of things that feel meaningful but require no meaningful change in how you allocate your time or money: 'be aware,' 'start conversations,' 'educate yourself.' The list below is not that. It is organized from smallest to largest commitment, and it is honest about which items require actual effort.

At the information level: Read the primary sources, not just the summaries. Piketty's Capital in the Twenty-First Century is long and worth the effort. Saez and Zucman's The Triumph of Injustice (2019) is shorter and specifically focused on U.S. tax policy. Anand Giridharadas's Winners Take All, covered in Chapter Eight, is the most accessible treatment of how elite philanthropy captures the terms of the social change debate. The reason to read primary sources rather than summaries is that primary sources make it harder to dismiss the argument as political rather than empirical. The data is the data.

At the money level: Where your money goes is a vote for what kind of institutions exist. Banking with a community development financial institution rather than a megabank is not going to restructure American finance, but it directs your deposits toward community lending rather than proprietary trading. Choosing to shop at employee-owned or worker-cooperative businesses when available is the same logic applied to retail. These are not solutions. They are what people with limited time and money can do while the structural work happens at other levels. They matter less than is sometimes claimed and more than doing nothing.

At the civic level: Local and state policy is where wealth concentration is most directly addressable in the current political environment, and it is where individual civic participation has the most leverage. Property tax policy, zoning regulations, local minimum wage ordinances, state inheritance tax structures, public university funding levels: these are all governed at levels where organized constituents can move outcomes. School board elections and city council races are decided by margins that individual civic engagement affects. The people who benefit from current arrangements understand this and invest in local politics accordingly. The people who don't benefit often don't show up for local elections in numbers that match their stakes.

At the organizing level: The Nordic evidence and the New Deal evidence converge on a single finding that the policy debate often underweights: labor institutions matter more than tax policy for pre-distribution outcomes. Wage compression in the Nordic countries is achieved primarily through coordinated bargaining systems with strong union participation, not primarily through tax-and-transfer redistribution. In the United States, union membership fell from approximately one-third of the workforce when Reagan took office to around 10 percent today. That decline corresponds directly to the divergence between productivity growth and median wage growth over the same period. Supporting labor organizing, financially, through consumer choices with unionized businesses, through political participation in elections and ballot initiatives that affect labor law, is the structural intervention with the longest documented historical track record. It is also the one most actively and expensively opposed by concentrated wealth, which is itself informative about its leverage.

At the political level: The interventions described in this chapter (progressive wealth taxation, estate tax reform, corporate governance requirements, and campaign finance disclosure are not fringe positions. They have majority support in polling across party identification when described in concrete terms rather than ideological framing. They are blocked not by public opposition but by the institutional capture of the legislative process by concentrated wealth. The most direct response to institutional capture is not cynicism (cynicism is free and changes nothing), but organized political participation in primaries, in ballot initiatives, and in the funding of candidates who are not beholden to concentrated donor interests. This is harder and slower than the other items on the list. It is also the only one that changes the pipe rather than managing the flood.

The research in this book is not a reason for despair. It is a map. Maps don't move you. But you can't find the destination without one.

Earned Optimism

The final pages of a book about wealth pathology have an obligation not to leave the reader in a well-documented swamp with no sense of direction. So here is the honest version of optimism, not the naive kind that waves away the difficulty, but the earned kind that comes from knowing the history.

The system that produces the patterns this book describes is not ancient or immovable. The extreme wealth concentration of the current moment is historically recent. As recently as the mid-1970s, the United States had a substantially more equal distribution of income and wealth, stronger labor institutions, and a political environment in which the policy instruments for addressing inequality were considered normal rather than radical. That changed through specific policy choices, specific political campaigns, and specific institutional investments over roughly four decades. It can change back through the same mechanisms operating in the other direction. The timeline is not short. The mechanisms are not simple. But the precedent for a different arrangement is sitting there in living memory.

The wealth pathology documented in this book is also not universal. The research on hubris syndrome, on power-disinhibition, on entitlement and empathy erosion documents tendencies and statistical associations, not deterministic outcomes. There are wealthy people who maintain relational integrity, who use power in ways that empower others rather than concentrating it further, who fund systemic change rather than buying reputation insurance. They are not the majority in the research literature, but they exist, and their existence proves the syndrome is not chemically inevitable. The question is whether the institutional environment makes those outcomes more or less likely, and whether structural change can shift the distribution toward them.

Finally: the fact that this information is now widely accessible is itself a development. The research on DARVO exists and is free to read. The empirical work on wealth concentration exists and is public. The historical analysis of what policy changes produced what distributional outcomes exists and is documented. The previous generation of people experiencing the dynamics this book describes did not have a name for DARVO. They did not have Piketty's 700-page empirical history of capital accumulation. They did not have the neuroscience of power disinhibition or the psychology of entitlement. The growing body of accessible research on these dynamics is a form of collective cognitive infrastructure that makes collective action more possible than it has been before.

Knowledge without strategy is just anger, as this book's outline noted early on. But anger without knowledge is blind. The research in these eleven chapters is not a reason to be more angry. It is a reason to be more precise about what is happening, more strategic about what might change it, and more grounded in the evidence about what has actually worked when the water level came down before.

The pipe is findable. Other people have found it. The work is in the turning.

The Wealth Insanity Cycle was not assembled overnight, and it will not be disassembled overnight. But it was assembled by people making specific decisions under specific incentive structures, and the historical record contains clear examples of what it looks like when those incentive structures are changed by collective political will. The Cycle is a machine. Machines can be turned off. The question is who controls the switch, and how they got there.

Notes

The following notes are organized by chapter. Each note corresponds to a research finding, quotation, or claim made in the chapter text. Where a source is cited in multiple chapters, it appears in full at first use and as a short form in subsequent references.

Chapter One: Your Brain on Money

Primary Studies

1. Hogeveen, Jeremy, Michael Inzlicht, and Sukhvinder S. Obhi. 'Power Changes How the Brain Responds to Others.' Journal of Experimental Psychology: General 143, no. 2 (2014): 755–762. https://doi.org/10.1037/a0033477. TMS study at Wilfrid Laurier University showing high-power priming reduces motor resonance, the neural mechanism underlying social mirroring.

2. Piff, Paul K., Daniel M. Stancato, Stéphane Côté, Rodolfo Mendoza-Denton, and Dacher Keltner. 'Higher Social Class Predicts Increased Unethical Behavior.' Proceedings of the National Academy of Sciences 109, no. 11 (2012): 4086–4091. https://doi.org/10.1073/pnas.1118373109. Correction issued 2017: https://doi.org/10.1073/pnas.1716910114. Seven-study investigation: driving behavior, candy experiments, negotiation

lying, and attitudes toward greed across 1,000+ participants.

3. Stellar, Jennifer E., Vida M. Anderson, Dacher Keltner, and Michael W. Kraus. 'Class and Compassion: Socioeconomic Factors Predict Responses to Suffering.' Emotion 12, no. 3 (2012): 449–459. https://doi.org/10.1037/a0026508. UC Berkeley study; upper-class participants showed reduced physiological compassion response to suffering.

4. Berridge, Kent C., and Terry E. Robinson. 'What Is the Role of Dopamine in Reward: Hedonic Impact, Reward Learning, or Incentive Salience?' Brain Research Reviews 28, no. 3 (1998): 309–369. https://doi.org/10.1016/S0165-0173(98)00019-8. Foundational research distinguishing the dopamine-driven 'wanting' system from the opioid-driven 'liking' system.

5. Volkow, Nora D., Joanna S. Fowler, and Gene-Jack Wang. 'The Addicted Human Brain: Insights from Imaging Studies.' Journal of Clinical Investigation 111, no. 10 (2003): 1444–1451. https://doi.org/10.1172/JCI18533. PET imaging establishing dopamine reward circuitry as shared neural substrate for addiction; tolerance as predictable neuroadaptation.

Books

6. Keltner, Dacher. The Power Paradox: How We Gain and Lose Influence. New York: Penguin Press, 2016. Two decades of behavioral power research including the Cookie Monster experiment.

7. Dutton, Kevin. The Wisdom of Psychopaths: What Saints, Spies, and Serial Killers Can Teach Us About Success. New York: Scientific American/Farrar, Straus and Giroux, 2012.

Chapter Two: Power Poisoning

Primary Studies

8. Owen, David, and Jonathan Davidson. 'Hubris Syndrome: An Acquired Personality Disorder? A Study of US Presidents and UK Prime Ministers over the Last 100 Years.' Brain 132, no. 5 (2009): 1396–1406. https://doi.org/10.1093/brain/awp008. Formally proposed hubris syndrome as an acquired personality disorder; 14 clinical criteria mapped across a century of heads of government.

9. Owen, David. 'Hubris Syndrome.' Clinical Medicine 8, no. 4 (2008): 428–432. https://doi.org/10.7861/clinmedicine.8-4-428. Earlier formulation establishing that hubris syndrome manifests after sustained power and largely resolves when power ends.

10. Hambrick, Donald C., and Phyllis A. Mason. 'Upper Echelons: The Organization as a Reflection of Its Top Managers.'

Academy of Management Review 9, no. 2 (1984): 193–206. https://doi.org/10.5465/amr.1984.4277628. Foundational upper-echelons theory establishing CEO characteristics as predictive of organizational outcomes.

11. Hambrick, Donald C., and Gregory D. S. Fukutomi. 'The Seasons of a CEO's Tenure.' Academy of Management Review 16, no. 4 (1991): 719–742. https://doi.org/10.5465/amr.1991.4279621. Five-stage lifecycle model of CEO tenure documenting cognitive rigidity and deteriorating decision quality over time.

12. Darouichi, Abdelaziz, Alain Klarsfeld, Jérôme Méric, and Richard Soparnot. 'CEO Tenure: An Integrative Review and Pathways for Future Research.' Corporate Governance: An International Review 29, no. 5 (2021): 658–683. https://doi.org/10.1111/corg.12396. Comprehensive review confirming Hambrick-Fukutomi model with contemporary empirical evidence.

13. Shi, Wei, Guoli Chen, and Brian L. Connelly. 'The Blind Power: Power-Led CEO Overconfidence and M&A Decision Making.' Journal of Business Research 109 (2020): 474–489. https://doi.org/10.1016/j.jbusres.2019.09.060. Sample of 13,754 US firm-year observations, 1996–2014; CEO power

predicts overconfidence which predicts value-destroying acquisitions.

Chapter Three: Psychopaths in Suits

Primary Studies

14. Babiak, Paul, Craig S. Neumann, and Robert D. Hare. 'Corporate Psychopathy: Talking the Walk.' Behavioral Sciences & the Law 28, no. 2 (2010): 174–193. https://doi.org/10.1002/bsl.925. PCL-R assessment of 203 high-potential corporate professionals; psychopathic trait prevalence ~3.9%, nearly four times the general population rate.

15. Board, Belinda J., and Katarina Fritzon. 'Disordered Personalities at Work.' Psychology, Crime & Law 11, no. 1 (2005): 17–32. https://doi.org/10.1080/10683160310001634304. Senior British managers scored higher than Broadmoor psychiatric patients on histrionic, narcissistic, and compulsive personality disorder traits.

16. Boddy, Clive R. 'Corporate Psychopaths, Bullying and Unfair Supervision in the Workplace.' Journal of Business Ethics 100, no. 3 (2011): 367–379. https://doi.org/10.1007/s10551-010-0689-5. Corporate psychopaths in leadership associated with significantly higher workplace bullying rates and reduced employee well-being.

Books

17. Hare, Robert D. Without Conscience: The Disturbing World of the Psychopaths Among Us. New York: Guilford Press, 1993. Reprint, 1999.

18. Hare, Robert D. Manual for the Revised Psychopathy Checklist. 2nd ed. Toronto: Multi-Health Systems, 2003.

19. Babiak, Paul, and Robert D. Hare. Snakes in Suits: When Psychopaths Go to Work. New York: HarperCollins, 2006. Revised edition, 2019.

Chapter Four: This Isn't New

Primary Sources

20. Watts, Edward J. Mortal Republic: How Rome Fell into Tyranny. New York: Basic Books, 2018. Primary source for Roman Republic material; Watts explicitly connects elite behavioral failure to institutional erosion.

21. Veblen, Thorstein. The Theory of the Leisure Class: An Economic Study of Institutions. New York: Macmillan, 1899. Available via Project Gutenberg. Introduced 'conspicuous consumption,' 'conspicuous leisure,' and 'pecuniary emulation.'

22. Josephson, Matthew. The Robber Barons: The Great American Capitalists, 1861–1901. New York: Harcourt, Brace, 1934. Reprint, New York: Harvest Books, 1962.

23. Twain, Mark, and Charles Dudley Warner. The Gilded Age: A Tale of Today. Hartford: American Publishing Company, 1873. Available via Project Gutenberg.

Secondary Sources

24. Beatty, Jack. Age of Betrayal: The Triumph of Money in America, 1865–1900. New York: Knopf, 2007.

25. Kiger, Patrick J. 'How Robber Barons Flaunted Wealth During the Gilded Age.' History.com, August 8, 2025. https://www.history.com/articles/robber-barons-gilded-age-wealth.

Chapter Five: The Empathy Gap

Primary Studies

26. Kraus, Michael W., Stéphane Côté, and Dacher Keltner. 'Social Class, Contextualism, and Empathic Accuracy.' Psychological Science 21, no. 11 (2010): 1716–1723. https://doi.org/10.1177/0956797610387613. Three studies demonstrating lower-class individuals outperform upper-class on empathic accuracy including standardized tests, live interactions, and reading emotions from photographs of eyes.

27. Stellar, Jennifer E., Vida M. Manzo, Michael W. Kraus, and Dacher Keltner. 'Class and Compassion: Socioeconomic Factors Predict Responses to Suffering.' Emotion 12, no. 3 (2012): 449–459.

https://doi.org/10.1037/a0026508. See note 3. The gap between verbal self-report of sadness and physiological response (heart rate deceleration) is the chapter's key methodological finding.

28. Piff, Paul K., Daniel M. Stancato, Stéphane Côté, Rodolfo Mendoza-Denton, and Dacher Keltner. 'Higher Social Class Predicts Increased Unethical Behavior.' See note 2.

29. Piff, Paul K. 'Wealth and the Inflated Self: Class, Entitlement, and Narcissism.' Personality and Social Psychology Bulletin 40, no. 1 (2014): 34–43. https://doi.org/10.1177/0146167213501699. Wealthier individuals score higher on narcissism and entitlement; experimentally inducing egalitarianism reduced narcissistic tendencies.

Neural and Physiological Evidence

30. Hogeveen, Jeremy, Michael Inzlicht, and Sukhvinder S. Obhi. 'Power Changes How the Brain Responds to Others.' See note 1.

Chapter Six: The Rules Are for You

Primary Case Material

31. Ethan Couch case documentation. Tarrant County, Texas. June 2013 crash; December 2013 sentencing. Wikipedia entry on Ethan Couch (retrieved March 2026). Key comparison: Eric Bradlee Miller: one death, BAC 0.11, sentenced to 20 years by the same judge who gave Ethan Couch 10

years' probation for four deaths and BAC 0.24. Documented legal record.

Primary Psychological Research

32. Bandura, Albert. 'Moral Disengagement in the Perpetration of Inhumanities.' Personality and Social Psychology Review 3, no. 3 (1999): 193–209. https://doi.org/10.1207/s15327957pspr0303_3. Foundational paper establishing eight mechanisms of moral disengagement: moral justification, euphemistic labeling, advantageous comparison, displacement of responsibility, diffusion of responsibility, distortion of consequences, dehumanization, attribution of blame.

33. Bandura, Albert. Moral Disengagement: How People Do Harm and Live with Themselves. New York: Worth/Macmillan, 2016. Full-length synthesis applying the framework to corporate transgressions, financial sector behavior, and political violence.

34. Bandura, Albert, Gian Vittorio Caprara, and Laszlo Zsolnai. 'Corporate Transgressions through Moral Disengagement.' In Ethics in the Economy: Handbook of Business Ethics, edited by L. Zsolnai, 151–164. Oxford: Peter Lang, 2002. Direct application to organizational misconduct.

Chapter Seven: Sex, Power, and Why This Keeps Happening

Primary Studies

35. Bargh, John A., Paula Raymond, John B. Pryor, and Fritz Strack. 'Attractiveness of the Underling: An Automatic Power-Sex Association and Its Consequences for Sexual Harassment and Aggression.' Journal of Personality and Social Psychology 68, no. 5 (1995): 768–781. https://doi.org/10.1037/0022-3514.68.5.768. Power primes automatically activate sexual associations below conscious awareness threshold.

36. Keltner, Dacher, Deborah H. Gruenfeld, and Cameron Anderson. 'Power, Approach, and Inhibition.' Psychological Review 110, no. 2 (2003): 265–284. https://doi.org/10.1037/0033-295X.110.2.265. Foundational approach-inhibition theory: power activates behavioral approach while reducing inhibition.

37. Lammers, Joris, Janka I. Stoker, Jennifer Jordan, Monique Pollmann, and Diederik A. Stapel. 'Power Increases Infidelity Among Men and Women.' Psychological Science 22, no. 9 (2011): 1191–1197. https://doi.org/10.1177/0956797611416252. 1,561-professional survey; organizational power predicts infidelity equally across genders, a power story, not a gender story. Note: Stapel subsequently

found to have fabricated data in other studies; independent replications of the core power-infidelity finding have supported the relationship.

38. Lammers, Joris, and Jon K. Maner. 'Power and Attraction to the Counternormative Aspects of Infidelity.' Journal of Sex Research 53, no. 1 (2016): 54–63. https://doi.org/10.1080/00224499.2014.989483. Power's infidelity association mediated by attraction to transgression, not additional opportunity.

Chapter Eight: The Philanthropy Con

Primary Psychological Research

39. Merritt, Anna C., Daniel A. Effron, and Benoît Monin. 'Moral Self-Licensing: When Being Good Frees Us to Be Bad.' Social and Personality Psychology Compass 4, no. 5 (2010): 344–357. https://doi.org/10.1111/j.1751-9004.2010.00263.x. Foundational review distinguishing moral credits (balancing) from moral credentials (reinterpretation); the latter is the philanthropy mechanism.

40. Mazar, Nina, and Chen-Bo Zhong. 'Do Green Products Make Us Better People?' Psychological Science 21, no. 4 (2010): 494–498. https://doi.org/10.1177/0956797610363538. Green-shopping study illustrating licensing mechanism; replication results

mixed, cited here as illustration of mechanism, not settled finding.

41. Monin, Benoît, and Dale T. Miller. 'Moral Credentials and the Expression of Prejudice.' Journal of Personality and Social Psychology 81, no. 1 (2001): 33–43. https://doi.org/10.1037/0022-3514.81.1.33. Establishing non-prejudiced credentials licenses subsequent potentially prejudiced positions; directly relevant to philanthropic credential-building.

Policy and Financial Research

42. Baker Institute for Public Policy. 'Do Donor-Advised Funds Need More Regulation?' Issue Brief. Rice University, April 2024. https://www.bakerinstitute.org/research/do-donor-advised-funds-need-more-regulation. Contributions to DAFs grew 400% in recent years; majority of holders pay out less than 5% annually; a third gave nothing in a given year.

The payout gap has a human cost that the percentage figures obscure. According to the National Philanthropic Trust's 2023 Donor-Advised Fund Report, assets held in donor-advised fund accounts totaled over $229 billion as of 2022. If those funds were subject to the same five percent annual payout requirement as private foundations, approximately $11.5 billion additional dollars would flow to charitable causes each year. For context: the entire annual budget of the National Institutes of Health, the primary funder of American biomedical research, is approximately

$47 billion. The money sitting in donor-advised funds, undeployed, represents a significant fraction of the national research enterprise. It is not being used for the purposes its donors claimed when they took the tax deduction. It is being warehoused.

Critical Works

43. Giridharadas, Anand. Winners Take All: The Elite Charade of Changing the World. New York: Knopf, 2018.

44. Reich, Rob. Just Giving: Why Philanthropy Is Failing Democracy and How It Can Do Better. Princeton, NJ: Princeton University Press, 2018.

Chapter Nine: Inherited Crazy

Primary Developmental Psychology Research

45. Luthar, Suniya S. 'The Culture of Affluence: Psychological Costs of Material Wealth.' Child Development 74, no. 6 (2003): 1581–1593. https://doi.org/10.1046/j.0009-3920.2003.00625.x. Foundational synthesis: affluent youth show elevated anxiety, depression, and substance use driven by achievement pressure and parental isolation.

46. Luthar, Suniya S., and Shawn J. Latendresse. 'Children of the Affluent: Challenges to Well-Being.' Current Directions in Psychological Science 14, no. 1 (2005): 49–53. https://doi.org/10.1111/j.0963-

7214.2005.00333.x. Affluent suburban children showed no significant parenting-quality advantage over inner-city low-income children on core dimensions.

47. Luthar, Suniya S., and Bronwyn E. Becker. 'Privileged but Pressured? A Study of Affluent Youth.' Child Development 73, no. 5 (2002): 1593–1610. https://doi.org/10.1111/1467-8624.00492. Achievement pressure mechanism: overemphasis on accomplishment relative to character predicts adolescent depression, anxiety, and substance use.

48. Luthar, Suniya S., Samuel H. Barkin, and Elizabeth J. Crossman. ''I Can, Therefore I Must': Fragility in the Upper-Middle Classes.' Development and Psychopathology 25, no. 4pt2 (2013): 1529–1549. https://doi.org/10.1017/S0954579413000758.

49. Luthar, Suniya S., and Karen D'Avanzo. 'Contextual Factors in Substance Use: A Study of Suburban and Inner-City Adolescents.' Development and Psychopathology 11, no. 4 (1999): 845–867. https://doi.org/10.1017/S0954579499002357. Affluent suburban youth reported significantly higher substance use than inner-city peers, more strongly linked to psychological maladjustment.

Chapter Ten: How to Survive Them

Primary DARVO Research

50. Freyd, Jennifer J. 'Violations of Power, Adaptive Blindness, and Betrayal Trauma Theory.' Feminism & Psychology 7, no. 1 (1997): 22–32. https://doi.org/10.1177/0959353597071004. DARVO coined within betrayal trauma theory; the dependency dynamic explains why people remain in professionally harmful situations.

51. Harsey, Sarah J., Eileen L. Zurbriggen, and Jennifer J. Freyd. 'Perpetrator Responses to Victim Confrontation: DARVO and Victim Self-Blame.' Journal of Aggression, Maltreatment, and Trauma 26, no. 6 (2017): 644–663. https://doi.org/10.1080/10926771.2017.1320777. First empirical study of DARVO; higher DARVO exposure predicts greater victim self-blame and self-silencing.

52. Harsey, Sarah J., and Jennifer J. Freyd. 'Deny, Attack, and Reverse Victim and Offender (DARVO): What Is the Influence on Perceived Perpetrator and Victim Credibility?' Journal of Aggression, Maltreatment, and Trauma 29, no. 8 (2020): 897–916. https://doi.org/10.1080/10926771.2020.1774695. Key finding: education about DARVO before encountering it significantly mitigates its effects on observer judgment.

53. Harsey, Sarah J., Alexis A. Adams-Clark, and Jennifer J. Freyd. 'Associations Between Defensive Victim-Blaming Responses (DARVO), Rape Myth Acceptance, and Sexual Harassment.' PLOS ONE, 2024. https://doi.org/10.1371/journal.pone.0313642. DARVO use correlates with rape myth acceptance and harassment perpetration, reflecting stable accountability-avoidant worldview.

Chapter Eleven: Fix the System, Not the Symptoms

Historical Tax Policy and Inequality

54. Piketty, Thomas, Emmanuel Saez, and Gabriel Zucman. 'Distributional National Accounts: Methods and Estimates for the United States.' Quarterly Journal of Economics 133, no. 2 (2018): 553–609. https://doi.org/10.1093/qje/qjx043. Data source for effective tax rates for top 1% during 1950s (~16.9% effective income tax rate despite 91% nominal marginal rate).

55. Tax Foundation. 'Taxes on the Rich Were Not Much Higher in the 1950s.' Tax Policy Blog, February 2024. https://taxfoundation.org/data/all/federal/taxes-on-the-rich-1950s-not-high/. Engaged directly to avoid bumper-sticker version of historical argument; the nominal-vs-effective rate discrepancy is acknowledged honestly in the chapter text.

56. Living New Deal. 'Income and Wealth Taxes (1934–1941).' https://livingnewdeal.org/glossary/income-and-wealth-taxes-1934-1941/. Top marginal rate trajectory from 25% (1932) to 94% (1944). See also Thorndike, Joseph J. Their Fair Share: Taxing the Rich in the Age of FDR. Washington, DC: Urban Institute Press, 2013.

Nordic Model and Comparative Inequality

57. Blau, Francine D., and Lawrence M. Kahn. 'Income Equality in the Nordic Countries.' NBER Working Paper 33444. National Bureau of Economic Research, January 2025. https://www.nber.org/papers/w33444. Nordic income equality primarily driven by wage compression through coordinated bargaining, not primarily tax-transfer redistribution.

58. Jakobsen, Katrine, Kristian Jakobsen, Henrik Kleven, and Gabriel Zucman. 'Wealth Taxation and Wealth Accumulation: Theory and Evidence From Denmark.' Quarterly Journal of Economics 135, no. 1 (2020): 329–388. https://doi.org/10.1093/qje/qjz040. Denmark top 1% holds ~20% of wealth vs. ~40% US; gap widened from late 1990s onward.

Wealth Taxation Theory and Design

59. Piketty, Thomas. Capital in the Twenty-First Century. Translated by Arthur Goldhammer. Cambridge, MA: Harvard University Press, 2014.

60. Saez, Emmanuel, and Gabriel Zucman. The Triumph of Injustice: How the Rich Dodge Taxes and How to Make Them Pay. New York: W. W. Norton, 2019. Annual wealth tax rates of 2–8% on wealth above threshold; design critique of European wealth tax failures.

61. Piketty, Thomas, and Emmanuel Saez. 'A Theory of Optimal Inheritance Taxation.' Econometrica 81, no. 5 (2013): 1851–1886. https://doi.org/10.3982/ECTA10712.

Labor Institutions and Pre-Distribution

62. Freeman, Richard B., and James L. Medoff. What Do Unions Do? New York: Basic Books, 1984. Foundational empirical work on wage-compression and public-goods effects of union density.

About the Author

Paul Green is a corporate instructional designer, educator, and author with a master's degree who loves to make music. He writes across various areas of nonfiction, with a particular interest in the intersection of psychology, power, and human behavior.

www.ingramcontent.com/pod-product-compliance
Lightning Source LLC
LaVergne TN
LVHW010555110826
845149LV00003B/669

* 9 7 8 1 9 6 6 7 0 3 2 8 0 *